MW00353882

Dealing with the Tough Stuff

Dealing with the Tough Stuff

PRACTICAL SOLUTIONS FOR SCHOOL ADMINISTRATORS

John G. Gabriel
and
Paul C. Farmer

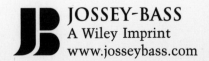

JOSSEY-BASS
A Wiley Imprint
www.josseybass.com

Copyright © 2012 by John Wiley & Sons, Inc. All rights reserved.

Published by Jossey-Bass
A Wiley Imprint
One Montgomery Street, Suite 1200, San Francisco, CA 94104-4594—www.josseybass.com

No part of this publication may be reproduced, stored in a retrieval system, or transmitted in any form or by any means, electronic, mechanical, photocopying, recording, scanning, or otherwise, except as permitted under Section 107 or 108 of the 1976 United States Copyright Act, without either the prior written permission of the publisher, or authorization through payment of the appropriate per-copy fee to the Copyright Clearance Center, Inc., 222 Rosewood Drive, Danvers, MA 01923, 978-750-8400, fax 978-646-8600, or on the Web at www.copyright.com. Requests to the publisher for permission should be addressed to the Permissions Department, John Wiley & Sons, Inc., 111 River Street, Hoboken, NJ 07030, 201-748-6011, fax 201-748-6008, or online at www.wiley.com/go/permissions.

Limit of Liability/Disclaimer of Warranty: While the publisher and author have used their best efforts in preparing this book, they make no representations or warranties with respect to the accuracy or completeness of the contents of this book and specifically disclaim any implied warranties of merchantability or fitness for a particular purpose. No warranty may be created or extended by sales representatives or written sales materials. The advice and strategies contained herein may not be suitable for your situation. You should consult with a professional where appropriate. Neither the publisher nor author shall be liable for any loss of profit or any other commercial damages, including but not limited to special, incidental, consequential, or other damages. Readers should be aware that Internet Web sites offered as citations and/or sources for further information may have changed or disappeared between the time this was written and when it is read.

Jossey-Bass books and products are available through most bookstores. To contact Jossey-Bass directly call our Customer Care Department within the U.S. at 800-956-7739, outside the U.S. at 317-572-3986, or fax 317-572-4002.

Wiley publishes in a variety of print and electronic formats and by print-on-demand. Some material included with standard print versions of this book may not be included in e-books or in print-on-demand. If this book refers to media such as a CD or DVD that is not included in the version you purchased, you may download this material at **http://booksupport.wiley.com**. For more information about Wiley products, visit **www.wiley.com**.

Front cover photo by Pesky Monkey/© iStockphoto

Library of Congress Cataloging-in-Publication Data

Gabriel, John G.
  Dealing with the tough stuff : practical solutions for school administrators / John G. Gabriel and Paul C. Farmer. – First edition.
       pages cm
     Includes bibliographical references and index.
  ISBN 978-1-118-13294-4 (paperback); ISBN 978-1-118-22511-0 (ebk.); 978-1-118-23862-2 (ebk.); 978-1-118-26321-1 (ebk.)
  1. School management and organization.   2. First year school principals.   I. Farmer, Paul C. II. Title.
  LB2805.G128 2012
  371.2–dc23
                              2012011846

Printed in the United States of America
FIRST EDITION
PB Printing   10 9 8 7 6 5 4 3 2 1

To the countless teachers and administrators who selflessly dedicate their lives to one of service: we have been honored to know and work with you, and we thank you for helping us become effective administrators.

CONTENTS

FOREWORD

This is the book I needed when I started teaching almost forty years ago. In order to be a good math teacher, I thought, I needed to know the Pythagorean Theorem somewhat better than my students. I needed to reward good performance and punish bad performance. I needed to keep parents happy and, most of all, keep the principal out of my classroom. What could possibly go wrong with this theory of teaching?

As Gabriel and Farmer incisively remind us, I was dead wrong in my early theories. While I was worrying about parents and principals, I was forgetting about students—the daily dramas of their lives and the real work of teaching and leadership that presented challenges far beyond ensuring that my students understood that the square of the hypotenuse was equal to the square of the two sides of a right triangle. In fact, as the authors forcefully write, the triangle most important to students is not that of Pythagoras but rather of friend, foe, and teacher in the drama of school. Although I continue to think that the Pythagorean Theorem is important, this book helps me understand that administrators and teachers would be well advised to pay as much attention to the friends and rivals of Pythagoras as to his theorem.

What can school leaders do to improve the school environment for students, teachers, and administrators? Prevailing opinions suggest a range of contradictory solutions, from improving teacher efficacy by employing greater levels of data analysis to relieving teachers' stress and anxiety by eliminating data analysis. Perhaps we should give students more freedom? No—let's restrict their choices so that they gain proficiency and defer their preferences until later. Shall we give school principals the discretion to respond to local needs, or create a consistent system of curriculum and assessment in the hopes that this will provide equity for all students within the system? Although strong arguments can be made for a variety of educational options, Gabriel and Farmer appeal to the more immediate needs of school administrators. The authors remind us that the imperative of improving schools in the real world is not always accomplished through strategic plans or gauzy vision statements. What school leaders need are practical solutions to address their most persistent challenge: *How can we engage students, teachers, and leaders today with maximum learning and minimum disruption?*

The answers, the authors suggest, include a consistent and practical set of protocols for responding to students, in which adults in the school model respectful responses to challenges. Their lessons extend far beyond classroom conflicts. (Indeed, their advice would be sound for many boardroom brawls I have witnessed.) Superintendents' cabinets, board meetings, and parent organizations would all benefit from these thoughtful protocols for dealing with disagreement and dissent.

This is an immensely practical book, providing a vital resource to new school administrators while at the same time helping veteran educators recognize that the remedies we used decades ago may not be as effective as we thought. I particularly appreciate the blend of twenty-first-century strategies, sensitive to digital natives, with tried-and-true methods for dealing with student disruptions, which respond to age-old motivational dynamics between students and teachers.

Although some of the advice in the book may strike the reader as common sense, most educators know that common sense is decidedly uncommon. "Just listen," the authors suggest, when my initial inclination is to lecture. "Don't bluff," these pages advise, when my instinct is that of the blowhard, full of bluster and blame. I wish I could say that I've learned every lesson that Gabriel and Farmer have to offer, but the simple truth is that all of us who work with adolescents and preadolescents must look in the mirror and acknowledge the chasm between what we know to be effective practice and our daily reality. That is precisely the reason that this book is so effective: it is born of practitioners. Although some readers may sigh and say, "What a blinding flash of the obvious!" other observers will wonder why such seemingly obvious findings are not more commonly reflected in our collective professional practices.

Finally, the authors remind us that the essential communication is not only with students but also with colleagues. These are not easy conversations, but they are critically important. Respect, challenge, and recognition of the reality that our colleagues face on a daily basis will be the hallmarks of communication that is meaningful and effective. Leaders will be challenged to acknowledge their own roles in improving staff effectiveness, and staff members will be challenged with the certainty that their actions and commitments are vital to improved student learning. This balance will be unsettling to some readers, as blame is far more comfortable than acceptance of responsibility. Nevertheless, the following pages will challenge educators at every level, from the board room to the classroom, to embrace responsibility for improved relationships and results.

Douglas Reeves
Founder, The Leadership and Learning Center
Author of more than thirty books and many articles
2010 recipient of the National Staff Development Council's
Contribution to the Field award
Boston, Massachusetts

ACKNOWLEDGMENTS

John Gabriel

Numerous people have had an impact on me. I am a culmination of each person's advice, suggestions, and guidance, and for that I am grateful, but also at a loss as to how to begin thanking people in such a short amount of space. With that said, I am blessed to have a wonderful and supportive family, as well as extended family; I am appreciative of their encouragement and support. I am especially grateful to and indebted to my wife, Caroline, for her understanding, patience, and vigorous support of me, my goals, and, quite plainly, what needs to be done. Similarly, I thank my parents not only for their patience but also for instilling in me a love for reading and writing at such a young age.

There are many colleagues whom I would like to thank. I have mentioned many of these individuals in previous books, so I would rather not repeat them all here, but suffice it to say that you have helped me grow and learn in a great many ways, and I would not be where I am today without your help. Here I thank Dr. Edgar Hatrick, Sharon Ackerman, and Mary Ann Hardebeck for their support and inspiring leadership; David Spage, whose perspective, insight, and opinions I value; Jennifer Piccolomini, a talented rising administrator who has seen and grown so much in a short period of time; Joseph Breinig Jr. for being so knowledgeable; Jeffrey Rounsley for making it look easy with his sharp insight and ideas and especially for his help with unpacking the World History SOL; and Allison Boyle, Jessica Pendleton, and Charles Barrett for helping me along and teaching me so much in such a short period of time. I am also thankful for having such a supportive network of principals both within and outside Loudoun County. Special thanks also to the review panel who previewed this text: your guidance and suggestions helped turn the manuscript around. Also, both Paul and I are grateful to Marjorie McAneny and Tracy Gallagher of Jossey-Bass for their support and patience during this process. In addition, we appreciate and applaud Michele Jones's sharp eye and deft handle on the written word. Finally, I continue to be impressed and inspired by Paul Farmer, whose perspective and approach still shape me.

Paul Farmer

I owe gratitude to so many people in my life: certainly my family, who have always been there through better and worse with belief, support, and encouragement no matter what my next adventure or project has been. They are patient as I allow my work and research to be placed before their needs, but they are skillful in making sure that I maintain a balance. In addition, I have been blessed with several opportunities to partner with hundreds of talented educators in Montgomery County, Maryland, and Fairfax County, Virginia. We worked together side by side while reaching the highest levels of learning possible, not just for students but for us as well.

Since leaving the school system as a full-time employee, I have been humbled over and again by opportunities to work and to share experiences with thousands of educators. So often they say how good I am, and I try to consistently reply that my work today is a reflection of those with whom I have worked: they—not I—are the ones who are so good.

I would be remiss if I didn't recognize my most current team of education partners at Solution Tree. My time as an associate with them is unmatched: I am surrounded by incredible people, support, and ideas that continue to challenge how we will grow as a national icon for professional development. I also acknowledge Jessica Lewis from Fairfax County Public Schools for her perspective as an elementary school administrator. And in regard to my closest education partner, John Gabriel, a person with the patience and the persistence to keep me focused long enough to complete a project like this: a thank you to John just doesn't say enough.

With so much support from so many, I can't name them all, but what tremendous assets they have all been in so many ways. For if they were not willing to challenge their practices and simultaneously challenge mine, I wouldn't have the skills to be where I am today.

ABOUT THE AUTHORS

John Gabriel is author of the best-selling book *How to Thrive as a Teacher Leader* (ASCD, 2005), which has also experienced success as a Chinese-translated text, *What It Takes to Make a Teacher Leader* (EQ, 2005); and coauthored *How to Help Your School Thrive Without Breaking the Bank* (ASCD, 2009) with Paul Farmer. A nationally and internationally known presenter, Gabriel recently opened and is the principal of John Champe High School in Loudoun County, Virginia. Prior to holding this position, he had been an assistant principal for seven years at Park View High School (Loudoun, Virginia), a minority-majority school that achieved the distinction of being a NASSP/MetLife Breaking Ranks School in 2010, an award given to only ten schools nationwide that year.

Gabriel's previous experience includes working as a department chair at Falls Church High School (Fairfax, Virginia), an extremely diverse school both ethnically and economically, where his dynamic leadership and transformation of the culture and climate of the department helped it reach levels of achievement on high-stakes assessments that had previously been unattainable. He can be reached at gabrielresearch@msn.com.

Paul Farmer, a nationally recognized expert consultant on professional learning communities (PLCs), is the coauthor of *How to Help Your School Thrive Without Breaking the Bank* (ASCD, 2009) and has thirty years of education experience. Currently Farmer works as an associate with Solution Tree, Inc., where he has provided consulting services on PLCs in more than forty states, three provinces, and the Northwest Territory in Canada. He provides professional development to create and sustain PLCs for teachers, school administrators, and district administrators, as well as gives keynote speeches and conducts training sessions through interactive videoconferencing.

Before becoming a consultant, Farmer worked for Fairfax County Public Schools in Virginia and Montgomery County Public Schools in Maryland. Before working as a director of instructional technology integration, Farmer was the principal of Joyce Kilmer Middle School (Fairfax), one of the first schools in the county to build a PLC and which was also recognized by Standard and Poor's School Evaluation Services for narrowing the achievement gap for economically disadvantaged students. As an educator in Montgomery County, Farmer served as classroom teacher, team leader, department chair, teacher specialist, and assistant principal. He can be reached at pcfarmer@learn4schools.com, and readers can follow him on Twitter (@pcfarmersr).

INTRODUCTION

No different from effective teachers, skillful administrators are ones who regularly seek ways to continue their growth. They are savvy enough, resourceful enough, and humble enough to understand that school administration is fraught with many challenges, complexities, and demands that are rarely addressed in preparatory programs and some that are even unknown to the administrator until he or she spends time in that position. If you are reading this book, then you are one such school leader who values tapping additional resources, finding and sharing ideas, techniques, and strategies to complement your repertoire to make some of the more difficult aspects of school administration seem less challenging.

If you are an aspiring administrator taking the requisite courses or even if you have completed the necessary credits to be an administrator, we commend you for exploring this professional path: your tentative first steps will help mitigate the impending shortage of school administrators. If you are a novice administrator, which we qualify as being in your first few years of service, we welcome you to a fulfilling and rewarding career of endless possibilities; it is a demanding one, but we have both found it to be richly satisfying. And if you are an experienced administrator, then we applaud your continued leadership in the service of others—the impact, both direct and indirect, that you have had on others' lives certainly exceeds the scope and impact you could have had as a classroom teacher. And your years of service have taught you that there is more to school administration than the mechanics of performing observations, writing evaluations, being knowledgeable about legal issues, and understanding leadership and management theory. All these topics certainly have an important place in preparatory programs and form a foundation for your leadership capacity, but you also understand that there is a larger-than-life reality to working in a school. Simply said, you often deal with the tough stuff: the nuts and bolts, the ins and outs of issues for which guidance isn't or wasn't always available.

The drive behind this book springs from that idea: that there was just so much we didn't realize as aspiring administrators, didn't learn upon completion of our preparatory programs, and wouldn't have known even as veteran administrators unless a mentor or colleague shared it with us. Although we graduated from excellent preparatory programs, the practical solutions to help us navigate the reality of daily challenges were acquired from practitioners in the field and learned on the job, not in the classroom. We therefore feel a kinship with you regardless of the stage of your career, and offer this book as another resource to aid you in managing and leading your school through the tough stuff.

With that in mind, this book is not a fix-all book, nor does it cover every aspect of administration. We've made a conscious decision not to cover those areas traditionally addressed in preparatory programs; rather, we have compiled a list of some of the more frequently occurring challenging aspects we've encountered as school administrators as well as those based on our experiences working with other administrators around the world.

Dealing with the Tough Stuff is divided into two sections: working with students and working with adults. You do not need to go through the book sequentially; the chapters and sections are not rigidly ordered, so feel free to move from one part of the book to the other to best meet your needs. It is our hope that upon reading it, you will share the ideas that we have culled from colleagues, from years of experience, and from trial and error with *your* colleagues, sparking a dialogue and enabling you to receive ideas in return from them—giving you more solutions for dealing with the tough stuff.

Dealing with the Tough Stuff

PART ONE

Working with Students

Responding to Student Conflicts

*Y*ou *had heard some rumblings a couple of weeks ago about two best friends who'd had a falling out. Once sworn friends, the two girls could no longer pass each other in the hall without their iciness having a polarizing effect across the school. The tension between the two was evident in classes, among cliques, and online. Even extracurricular activities weren't immune to the fallout; sides were taken and lines were drawn around the school, unbeknownst to you. You hadn't paid much attention to the initial conflict because you naïvely mistook the quiet for calm; how were you to know that the quiet was just the harbinger of the coming storm?*

And so when two shrill voices rose above the din of the class change one Monday morning while you were on hall duty, you really didn't understand what was occurring. When you arrived at the scene of the disturbance, you discovered the two girls pointing angrily in each other's faces, obscenities flying, and a crowd of onlookers rapidly getting sucked into the black hole the opponents were creating. Thankfully, no punches were thrown—there wasn't even a shove—but there was no mistaking the potential for violence or the disruption to the learning environment. Nor was there any mistaking the serious consequences that would have been handed out if there had been a physical conflict, or how two young adults unable to control wild and deep emotions would have jeopardized their otherwise well-respected academic records.

Life is marked by conflict. Whether it is between spouses, siblings, friends, or coworkers, conflict is a staple of the human condition. Of course, life is no different for your students than it is for you or for us. And given students' youth and inexperience, especially when coupled with the social environment of school and technology, student conflicts can easily, quickly, and frequently erupt. Their aftershocks can have a profound impact on social circles and the atmosphere in the school; and just when you think everything is quiet, tremors rippling beneath the surface initiate a whole new dramatic event. So it is only natural that many times over the course of a marking period, conflicts of all types and kinds eventually find their way to your office. And although these conflicts are a normal and necessary part of learning and growing up, their potential to cause such upheaval cannot be ignored.

RECOGNIZE STUDENT CONFLICTS

Student conflicts take a variety of shapes and forms. Some start innocently enough as simple disagreements and end there, never escalating into anything more significant. On the other end of the spectrum, though, are those that foment and culminate in verbal altercations (or worse), and they usually seem to occur anywhere and whenever there is an audience present—in the hallways, in the cafeteria, or while boarding buses, where the screaming, yelling, and cursing are heard by a significant portion of the school's population. Following are examples of the different types of conflicts you are bound to encounter in a secondary school setting.

Conflicts Caused by Rumor and Gossip

We find that most conflicts stem from something that someone has said behind the other person's back, either innocently or maliciously. Some students are very open and "share their business" with anyone who will listen, but then are surprised when everyone seems to be talking about their business or recent activities. In other instances, the instigating action might not even occur within the school building; perhaps something was posted online, texted, or e-mailed the previous night, but by the morning, the key player or players are suddenly aware of what has occurred, which often has an impact on the learning environment.

Relationship Conflicts

Regardless of their grade level, academic performance, or social clique, students experience school as their very own soap opera, and the relationships around which their lives revolve change on a nearly daily basis. Best friends become ex-friends, friends date their friends' exes, good friends are "frenemies" who engage in subtle and not-so-subtle battles, and an endless cycle of hookups and breakups courses through our houses of learning. As a result, our needing to help friends repair their relationships is a constant. However, we recommend always avoiding mediating students involved in romantic relationships; entering this area would be opening the proverbial can of worms.

Personality Conflicts

As much as we would like all of our students to get along with one another, the reality of life is that people don't and won't like everyone they meet, nor are they liked by everyone. This might seem obvious enough to us, but to the outgoing, optimistic, and academically successful fifteen-year-old girl, it usually comes as a surprise when she discovers that someone dislikes her without any apparent reason. She can't comprehend why a classmate always seems to mutter things under her breath when she passes her in the hallway or why she "mean mugs" her (staring, glaring at her, shooting her dirty looks). And this exemplary young woman might suddenly find herself losing control of her emotions or doing things that she had never done before because this person seems to be "out to get her" for "no reason."

Conflicts Caused by Racial, Ethnic, or Gender Differences

As our society becomes more and more diverse, our students become more tolerant and understanding of diversity, but, paradoxically, we also encounter more conflict as a result of the increasing diversity. You can certainly expect the same to be true in your school, especially if it is experiencing a major change in its demographics. Similarly, students in recent years have begun to feel more comfortable about expressing their sexual and gender identity, and even though it appears that young adults are more tolerant and accepting of LGBT people, these individuals are still likely to face conflict as well.

Bullying

Although many of the aforementioned types of conflict can manifest as bullying, it is important to identify bullying (including cyberbullying) as a distinct type of conflict. Trying to resolve situations that involve bullying through mediation is not appropriate, for many reasons; we will address bullying later in a separate section.

MEDIATE STUDENT CONFLICTS

In many instances, students are able to work out their problems and conflicts on their own; however, there are just as many times when they are not, perhaps because they lack the necessary skills, maturity, or self-awareness. But because students will certainly continue to have these conflicts once they leave school, they need to learn how to communicate effectively, appropriately, and maturely with someone with whom they disagree.

We have found that by serving as mediators between students and trying to get to the root causes of the conflict, we can help students resolve differences before situations escalate, which in turn has a powerful and lasting impact on the students and the school as a whole. And although the results are difficult to measure quantitatively, engaging students in conflict mediation seems to reduce the possibility of violence; by extension, these proactive measures also reduce the number of suspensions and disciplinary consequences. But perhaps most important, through mediation students learn valuable life lessons and skills. And in our experience, many students we have mediated eventually ended up becoming friends, or they repaired their relationships, something that was unlikely to have happened for most of students had they been left to their own devices.

But just because you know that a conflict requires mediation does not mean that the students will be open to mediation. The specific situation and personalities involved often dictate how you will first present the idea of mediation. If you generally anticipate a favorable reply, you can give the students the illusion of choice by asking if they would like to try mediation—to take the opportunity to discuss their conflict in an objective setting, with you as a neutral facilitator to help them understand the issue at the core of the conflict and to resolve it. However, in other situations, you do not present mediation as an option; rather, you simply state that it will happen, with the implicit understanding that the alternative option is disciplinary consequences. In some cases, you will immediately recognize that the situation is so combustible that any attempt to mediate would end disastrously, so you don't even entertain the option. Regardless of how you introduce the idea, the following are some basic guidelines for the mediation process.

Set the Stage

Before you sit the students down together, talk with each of them separately about what they can expect from you when they enter the room and what you expect from them. Acknowledge that there may be a point during the session when they may be upset or angry; convey that it is acceptable to feel that way, but also express your expectation and your confidence that they will be able to "keep it together."

Set the students at a clear table, free of staplers or other items that could be easy to use as projectiles. Also be aware of the arrangement of the furniture in the meeting area, as well as the location of the quickest exit. Although you naturally hope that physical conflict is unlikely, taking these steps can be very important for your safety and the safety of the students. Last, it helps to meet in a neutral area when possible. For example, if you are the administrator for one student and not the other, you might want to consider meeting in an office other than either yours or your colleague's. You need both students to understand that there are no sides in the relationship nor in the process, that the only objective is an agreed-on outcome.

Establish Ground Rules

Because you will be entering a charged situation, it is especially important that you create a structure that facilitates dialogue. Because conflicts often arise or continue because communication is impossible or unwanted, you want to create a climate that allows for communication. It is equally important to attempt to protect the emotional well-being of both parties involved, and establishing ground rules is the way to do so. But even if you address ground rules individually with the students, it is still a good idea to mention them again once they are seated in the room. As a way to break the ice and reinforce your expectations, you might even have the students restate the ground rules at the onset of mediation. The following are some ground rules that we have found particularly helpful. (Depending on the degree of the need for mediation, you might choose to explain them in more positive terms, as we have indicated.)

- *No standing up (Remain seated)*. Students must remain seated, especially because suddenly standing up could be perceived as a sign of aggression.

- *No yelling (Stay calm)*. Students will certainly raise their voices because you and they are dealing with an emotionally charged situation, but make it clear that they are not to yell at each other. If they do, you need to immediately call a "time-out," and as a referee send them back to their proverbial corners until they have cooled down and are able to continue with the mediation.

- *No personal attacks (Be objective).* Because students are vulnerable and upset in these situations, you can expect there to be cursing sometimes, although you needn't condone it. Policing swearing is not the sword that we choose to fall on, but we do make it clear that the students are present to have a productive conversation; name-calling and other personal attacks, such as derogatory or insulting comments, will not be tolerated, as they will not help produce a resolution.

- *No using pronouns (Use each other's names).* It might seem strange at first, but we ask students not to refer to each other as "him" or "her." Referring to someone in the third person when he or she is present often conveys a feeling of rudeness and a degree of disrespect; you want to reach a common ground, a process that starts first with demonstrating respect. By using each other's names, the students are forced not only to show a measure of respect but to acknowledge each other as an actual person. Personalizing the dialogue in this way can sometimes make it uncomfortable for students to continue to treat each other poorly.

- *No interrupting (Allow each other to speak).* Announce that each student will have the opportunity to tell his or her version of what happened. Acknowledge that they might not agree with the other's perception of what happened, but will be permitted to share their side of the situation without interruptions. Students will undoubtedly try to interrupt each other in order to defend themselves or to refute a claim, so in order to preserve the process and the other student's dignity, you will need to quickly and firmly signal that the interruption is out of line. You might even point out to the student that he was able to give his version without interruption, so now he needs to extend that same courtesy to the other party. If you see that the students really want to interrupt, you can suggest that they write their thoughts on a piece of note paper and use that as a guide to their part of the discussion. This suggestion indicates that you know that what they have to say is important to them, but that you still value adhering to the ground rules.

- *No blaming (Identify how you feel).* Have students avoid saying what the other person *did.* Instead, have them speak in terms of how they themselves *felt.* Although we understand that this is not always possible, realistic, or easy to monitor over the course of a charged conversation, encourage students to say things like, "I feel hurt and angry when you say things to me when I pass you in the hall" instead of "You say things to me in the hall" and so on. These kinds of "I statements" are usually perceived as less accusatory and combative and are less likely to put the listener on the defensive. In addition, this kind of framework allows the speaker to identify the cause of the conflict as well as what she is feeling, both of which are helpful to her and the other party involved in the mediation.

• *No arm-crossing or other negative body language (Be seen as positive).* What you should be concerned with here is minimizing body language and nonverbal gestures that could be perceived as defensive or offensive and instead encouraging those that would seem to indicate that the participants are listening. Ask students to sit up in their chairs and keep their hands on the table in order for them to listen better to what the other has to say. Whenever possible, try to have the students look at one another, as staring away or looking down could be interpreted as a sign of disrespect or disinterest.

It might seem that we are creating too rigid an environment in which to facilitate dialogue, and on some level, that may be true, which is why we encourage you to determine what works best for you and for your students. In our experience, we have found that a clearly defined structure is the foundation that leads to a mediation's success. You want to create an environment where students can be honest and expressive yet also come to a resolution without having the situation escalate.

Facilitate the Mediation

We don't have a prescription for determining which student should tell her version first, but you do stand a good chance of creating an unproductive environment if you select the "wrong" person to start. You might ask who would like to volunteer to begin the conversation, or flip a coin or utilize some other impartial way to begin the dialogue. In some cases where you know the students extremely well, when you speak with them privately you might explain why you will be letting the other person speak first, that she will be allowed to have the last word, and so on. For example, you might tell one student that because you trust her restraint and maturity, you are going to let the other student go first. Regardless of who begins the process, the following are some points to consider to help you facilitate the mediation.

Ask, "Why Are We Here?"   For the most part, you should already be familiar with the major plot points of the conflict, and you would have used this information to determine whether mediation would be an appropriate course of action. Regardless, you can open the mediation by simply asking the students, "Why don't you describe for me what happened?" or "Why are we are here?" It is crucial that each student be given an opportunity to share his or her perception of what the issue is.

Ask Open-Ended Questions   As much as possible, ask questions that set the stage for elaboration and description. If the goal of mediation is to get your students talking to one another (and, by extension, listening to one another as well), then detailed, expressive responses are your objective during the initial stages of the mediation process. Closed questions, to which students simply respond with yes, no, or some other one-word response, will not help you get closer to the root of the problem or to resolving it. You might also ask students to explain *how* they feel rather than having them *confirm* how they feel. But even with open-ended questions, you may discover you still need to coax the parties along with words of encouragement or other affirmations that put them at ease as well as assure them that someone is at least listening.

Verify and Ask Questions   Either along the way or when one student has finished sharing his version of the story, verify the main points. You should ask questions where something seems unclear (or even if it is clear, but for the benefit of the other student), summarize what has been said, and, where appropriate, inquire as to how the student felt as a result of whatever the action was.

Have Students Seek Clarification   Each student should be given the chance to ask the other clarifying questions. After the student shares his version of what the problem is, ask the other student if he has any questions he wants to ask. Be forewarned: this is a potentially explosive moment in the process because one student has had to sit quietly while the other had the opportunity to share his thoughts, so he can potentially be defensive, angry, and upset. You could also wait to have students ask questions after they have each had the chance to say what happened, but regardless of the timing, students need to have the chance to clarify what has been said. You may want to encourage the student to start and end the question with, "What I heard you say was . . . Is that correct?"

Remain Neutral   Because you are the authority figure in the room, many students will look to you as an arbiter, not as a mediator. They might not understand that your role is to facilitate a dialogue in a safe setting to come to a mutually satisfactory outcome, and not to dispense a decision or judgment. We are confident that you are professional enough to remain neutral and not take a side or agree with one student over another. However, there is still a chance that you could unknowingly and unintentionally convey partiality to one of the parties through simple word choices of which you might not even be aware. Johnson and Johnson (1995) offer the example that rather than saying, "She is angry because you stole her purse," you should instead say, "She is angry because you have her purse" (p. 81). In the latter statement, you are not accusing the student or judging her by saying, or agreeing with the other student, that she stole the purse. You are only stating a fact: she was in possession of the purse. Paying attention to small word choices like this can help you avoid seeming as though you are taking sides.

Take a Time-Out   Feel free to take a time-out if things are getting heated or if no progress is being made. It's good to give your students a few minutes to collect their thoughts and process what has just transpired, so a time-out can be an effective strategy for moving mediation along. In some instances, you might even want to use the time-out as a pep talk of sorts: coaching, coaxing, and commending participants separately can help set the stage for when they return to the table.

Reverse Roles   Negotiating an equitable outcome can depend on both students' understanding each other's perspective. Because students rarely do understand the other person's perspective, you might have them either actively role-play the conflict as the other person or have them present the other's position (Johnson and Johnson, 1995).

Identify the Problem   We hope that through verifying, summarizing, and clarifying, you have been able to identify the problem and to enable the students to identify the problem. The tricky part is that you need to do so in a way that preserves your role as an impartial facilitator who is not seen as taking sides or playing favorites. Along the way, you might have the students identify some common ground, as that is usually helpful in coming to a resolution.

Identify the Solution   By the end of the mediation, students should be able to articulate a couple of different solutions; it is not your responsibility to develop one. In fact, even if they cannot generate a solution, we encourage you to refrain from offering one. It would be better for you to ask questions that might lead them to coming up with their own solution—that way, there will be more ownership, buy-in, and sense of responsibility (not to mention that jointly developing a solution, if they can, will only further reduce the barrier between them). However, you might find that sometimes students "become fixated on one possible agreement and are unable to think of alternatives," so your role is to help them "break this fixation" (Johnson and Johnson, 1995, p. 87). After a solution has been agreed on, you should reiterate and emphasize it to ensure that everyone is clear on the expectations from that point forward and that it is something they will abide by or support, even if they don't agree with it.

Solicit Thoughts   We recommend that before both students leave, you make one final call for them to share anything that is on their mind. Remind them that if there is anything else that they want to say or share, now is the time to do so, because from this point forward, you will consider the issue resolved, and therefore don't expect to hear anything more about it (and nor should either party).

Offer Advice   We generally refrain from offering a lot of advice during the actual mediation because students are so caught up in what they are feeling or what is being said that they probably won't be able to hear what we are saying. However, near the end of these sessions, we do offer some important advice: ignore what others might say after the mediation has occurred. We find it is necessary to explain to the involved students that everyone likes free entertainment, so they are likely to hear one of their friends later say something to them like, "Do you know what I heard Ben say that Sue said about . . ." Advise your students to simply tell their friends or acquaintances that they and the other student have worked things out, and then walk away. You will find that because your students might not always hear it at home, they need to be told that their friends don't always have their best interest in mind—a difficult concept for adolescents to comprehend. Most cannot imagine that their friends will try to push their buttons in order to wind them up and watch the ensuing drama, which they find entertaining. So encourage them to respond with something along the lines of "We squashed that beef, so I don't need to hear anything more about it," or "I'm over that, so I'd appreciate not hearing any more about it" when they encounter peers trying to stir the pot.

State Future Consequences   At the end of a mediation session, after students have shaken hands or at least come to some kind of truce or understanding, it is important also to inform them of what could happen if the conflict continues, reignites, or escalates in the future, especially after you have warned them to refrain from engaging in this behavior. Remind your students that if you have to see them again on this issue, they would now be in defiance of you and your expectations of them, and as a result there could very well be disciplinary consequences for (further) incidents related to this conflict. You may want to ask them to repeat what you just said about future occurrences to ensure that they heard you.

Praise Their Participation   It is important to reinforce that your students made a good choice by agreeing to mediation. In addition to praising them during the process, you can do so at the close of the mediation. Specifically, you should highlight their maturity, restraint, and composure, and you might even engage in a little self-deprecation by saying something like, "I don't know if I could do [have done] this, so I really appreciate and admire what the two of you have accomplished here today."

Follow Up   It is essential that at some point you follow up with the students you engaged in mediation. You don't need to bring the students together again, but you should talk with each of them to get his or her perspective on how things have been since you last worked with them and get a feel for any problems or potential issues.

It should go without saying, but it is worth emphasizing that you should contact the students' parents after the mediation (and in some prickly cases, you might even want to inform the parents in advance). Be up-front with the students about contacting their parents; assure them that you are looking forward to telling their parents how well they worked through their differences and that you're confident that their issue is moot now. You should explain to the parents what the infraction consisted of—what transpired and how it made it to your office, as well as how the mediation session went and your intention of following up with the students.

Most parents will be pleased not only that you contacted them but also that you refrained from giving out disciplinary consequences and tried to work with the students to help them learn how to resolve situations.

If there are future conflicts between the disputants or an escalation in the conflict, mediation is no longer a viable option. You might need to consider disciplinary consequences, and, in some cases, if the students have contact with one another during the day, you might have to consider changing their schedules. If the students have the same class together and you have other options with their schedules, you should consider changing both of their schedules so that they are not in the same class (or sharing the same lunch period or other school-created opportunities for interaction, with the exception of class changes). Again, in order to retain your neutrality, we encourage you to change both students' schedules if you need to change one.

ADDRESS BULLYING

When you were growing up, you might have experienced a bullying situation and were told that a bully was simply someone who was afraid or insecure. You might even have been told that it was just how kids act toward kids; if you just stood your ground or learned how to ignore it, everything would be fine because it was a rite of passage that everyone goes through. Even if you weren't a target of bullying yourself, we're confident that you can recall a victim of it and understand in hindsight the pain, hurt, frustration, and humiliation that bullying causes. And as it now turns out, experts, research, and even common sense indicate that these notions about bullying are inaccurate or are in some cases overly simplistic. Moreover, being a victim of bullying can have significant effects on the development of a child, including substance abuse issues, poor school attendance and grades, lowered self-confidence and self-esteem, and social withdrawal. In severe instances, victims "have increased thoughts about suicide [or what has come to be known as "bullycide," which is committing suicide as a result of being bullied] that may persist into adulthood" and are also "more likely to retaliate through extremely violent measures," according to www.stopbullying.gov. Because the hurt caused by bullying is so acute and the effects so profound for an adolescent, we categorize bullying as a different type of conflict found in schools.

According to a MetLife survey (2004–2005), 50 percent of the students surveyed in the 2004–2005 school year said they were bullied or teased as a new student (p. 50), and according to the U.S. Department of Health and Human Services in partnership with the Department of Education and the Department of Justice, "56% of students have personally witnessed some type of bullying at school" (www.stopbullying.gov). The Department of Education recognizes bullying as a critical issue because "bullying can be extremely damaging to students, can disrupt an environment conducive to learning, and should not be tolerated in our schools." Secretary of Education Arne Duncan further explains in "Secretary of Education Bullying Law and Policy Memo" (www.stopbullying.gov/references/white_house_conference/, p. 93) that "recent incidents of bullying have demonstrated its potentially devastating effects on students, schools, and communities and have spurred a sense of urgency among State and local educators and policymakers to take action to combat bullying." You should inquire what your school or district has done or is doing regarding bullying because "many states are now requiring schools to have anti-bullying policies in place" (Boynton and Boynton, 2005, p. 161).

Understanding Bullying

Simply put, bullying is abuse. It is a repeated pattern of behavior and actions intended to purposely hurt, scare, or intimidate someone. The bully-victim relationship is primarily characterized by an imbalance of power, whether that power is physical, social, or even simply perceived. A person or group then leverages this power by intentionally attempting to cause direct or indirect harm to someone who is perceived as physically, emotionally, or socially weaker. This behavior differs from general "meanness" because there is a pattern of "repetition: incidents of bullying happen to the same person over and over by the same person or group" (www.stopbullying.gov).

Bullies generally select targets because they appear to be weaker or don't fit in socially, or because of their physical appearance or differences in culture, ethnicity, or religion. Victims might also lack socially significant symbols (the current "in" clothing, or knowledge about current pop culture trends and so on). What is distressing is that many times students report that these attacks are invisible to adults. In some cases, teachers might excuse bullying as a case of "kids being kids"; parents might be blind to it because many students feel ashamed and embarrassed about being a victim and therefore are hesitant to talk about it. In other instances, the bullying can be so subtle or so quick that it goes unnoticed. To further complicate matters, it seems that educators can even be focused on the wrong bully.

The traditional view of a bully is that he is a loner, someone on the fringe. This kind of bully is often unpopular himself, or "socially marginalized," according to Rodkin (2011), quoting Farmer and others (2010): they "may be fighting against a social system that keeps them on the periphery" (p. 12). And although this view of the bully is valid, it is almost antiquated when one considers the other type that Rodkin identifies, drawing again on Farmer and others: the "socially connected bullies" (p. 12). This kind of bully contradicts the traditional notion of the loner or the outsider trying to gain entry into social circles. Rather, these bullies "have a variety of friends . . . and strengths such as social skills, athleticism, or physical attractiveness. Socially connected bullies tend to be proactive and goal-directed in their aggression" (p. 12). According to Goodwin (2011), these students are far from "the social outcasts" of our youth and are instead "often popular or semipopular social climbers. . . . Stated bluntly, many kids climb the social pyramid on the backs of other students, using ostracism, ridicule, and gossip to gain social status" (p. 82). In some cases, as fictionalized and depicted in movies such as *Mean Girls,* the bullying is a means toward simply maintaining social status. Rodkin concludes that "educators who exclusively target peripheral, anti-social cliques as the engine of school violence problems may leave intact other groups that are more responsible for mainstream peer support of bullying" (p. 15). To make matters even more difficult to grasp, there is almost no real profile of a bully, as "it transcends race, it transcends gender and it transcends family income. Bullying can occur in every community and in every school" (Susan Swearer, quoted in "Bullying, Cyberbullying and the Schools," 2010). In fact, in this interview in the *School Leadership Briefing,* Swearer goes on to identify a subgroup of bullies, those who are "also victimized . . . [and] often get in trouble for bullying others but educators don't necessarily recognize that they are also being victimized, whether by peers or at home or in their neighborhood."

As an administrator, you have an almost sacred obligation to ensure a physically and emotionally safe learning environment for your students and to help your teachers understand what bullying is and when it occurs. In the traditional sense, bullying manifests itself in the following two forms:

- *Verbal.* This form of bullying is more along the lines of what people would recognize as "picking on" someone, and includes overt coercion or putdowns and subtle manipulation through persistent rumors, gossip, and the threat of exclusion, with the outcome being to hurt the target emotionally. This form of bullying can also involve social isolation.

- *Physical.* This kind of bullying conjures the image of the schoolyard bully telling classmates what to do, beating someone up for lunch money, or anything that involves violence or the threat of violence. Although this kind of overt abuse and more serious examples of it still occur, the threat of physical violence can be subtle, such as a shoulder nudge or tripping in the halls, "bucking" at someone, or even "accidentally" knocking the books or materials out of someone's hands. However the bullying might occur, the intention is to instill visceral fear in the target and to demonstrate dominance through physical contact.

Regardless of how the bullying is perpetrated, "Schools and individual staff members can and should deal with bullies and bullying behavior in order to contribute to a safe and orderly school environment, one free of threat and intimidation" (Boynton and Boynton, 2005, p. 162). However, with the advent of cyberbullying, maintaining a safe and orderly environment is now even more difficult for administrators.

Understanding Cyberbullying

With monumental advances in technology that can better connect people and enrich lives, so too comes an ease with which bullies can torment and isolate victims. Cyberbullying, whereby the abuse and attacks occur or continue in cyberspace, is no less real than bullying that occurs in a physical setting. The U.S. Department of Health and Human Services (www.stopbullying.gov) categorizes cyberbullying as "sending mean, vulgar, or threatening messages or images; posting sensitive, private information about another person; pretending to be someone else in order to make that person look bad; and intentionally excluding someone from an online group." Cyberbullying can also include the uploading of embarrassing videos, the creation of fake social media profiles, or the distribution of doctored (or real) photos.

The anonymity and ease with which it can occur, as well as its ability to go viral, have led to cyberbullying's seemingly becoming more common. It has also captured the mainstream media's attention with the suicides of middle schooler Megan Meier in 2006 and college student Tyler Clementi in 2010, both of whom were cyberbullied.

Responding to Bullying

Bullying cannot be ignored. If you or a staff member witnesses it or are told about it and think that it will just stop, you are doing the victim a grave injustice (not to mention the serious consequences you could face if it were discovered that you had ignored it). You have a moral imperative to convey to your staff the importance of responding to incidents of bullying, which encompasses addressing the bully (and his or her parents), meeting with the victim (and at least contacting his or her parents), establishing schoolwide expectations, and possibly implementing a prevention program.

Meeting with the Victim   One of the first things you need to do is assure the victim that he is not at fault, that he did nothing wrong, that he did not deserve what happened to him, and that he was right to tell you (or another authority figure, if that is how you discovered the situation) about what has been happening; validate his feelings and reassure him that he is not alone in what he is experiencing. You might even pledge to him that you will be sure to address it with the bully; however, you should also be able to guarantee that you will not tell the bully that the victim had come to you and "snitched." You might also think about making him aware of resources available to him, such as his school counselor, support groups, or community resources. Last, you need to counsel the student on how to respond if there are future attacks from a bully. First and foremost, you should emphasize that he should not respond with violence, which will just escalate the situation and could result in bodily harm. You might also encourage him to use humor if possible or simply either to ignore the bully or agree with what the bully says and walk away, and then tell you or any other trusted adult in the building (Boynton and Boynton, 2005). You should also be sure to encourage the victim to tell a trusted adult or call the police if necessary if anything were to happen in the community.

Talking with the Victim's Parents   When parents learn that their child has been bullied, the issue does not end for them when you hang up the phone or show them out of your office. We've had parents ask what they should do when their child comes home, so we offer them some gentle guidance on what they are in store for and how to handle the situation. Most important is to emphasize that their child did nothing wrong, that he did nothing to encourage this kind of behavior, and that no one deserves to be treated in such a fashion. You should also encourage the parents to adopt the same approach with their child; it is critical for the child to hear from his parents that he is not at fault. The student's feelings may be complicated: in addition to the hurt caused by the bullying, he may feel a sense of relief now that an adult is aware of the situation, but he can simultaneously and paradoxically be frustrated and annoyed; he may also experience shame and embarrassment for having his administrator know what happened to him and having his parents learn about it, along with whatever awkward conversations or drama that might ensue as a result. In short, the student will need support and understanding. The parents' job is to be sensitive to his feelings and reassure him that whatever he feels is normal.

After being told about the bullying, many parents of victims are understandably quite upset. You need to keep them calm as best you can and advise them not to take matters into their own hands. Under no circumstances should you give out the contact information of the other student's parents, and you probably shouldn't even disclose the identity of the bully to the parents unless the victim was in serious danger. Discourage the parents from calling the bully's parents, as that can escalate the situation and increase the chance of the victim's parents losing control during such a conversation if the bully's parents are defensive or, worse yet, if the victim's parents discover that the bullying behavior had been learned at home. You might also explain that calling the bully's parents could have the unintended result of worsening the situation for their child. Instead, assure the parents that you will be meeting with the other parents and will follow up with them afterward.

In some instances, we've spoken with parents who have warned us that they will make sure that their child retaliates if the situation happens again. When this occurs, we assure them that we understand their frustration and why they are saying that, but we then caution them about encouraging their child to retaliate: even though their child is the victim, he can just as easily run afoul of school rules and regulations (as well as the law), so parents need to understand the possible ramifications. We also mention that if their child were to retaliate, there is the chance that he could suffer serious physical harm.

Meeting with the Bully   When you meet with the bully, you'll see that before he admits to any wrongdoing (if he does at all), he will ask "Who told you that?" or "Where did you hear that from?" His purpose in asking is twofold: he's trying to determine exactly what it is that you know and how much, and at the same time, he's probing to find out if the victim "snitched" on him. In our experience, if you are dismissive of his questions and respond with something like "Don't worry how I heard this" or "That's none of your business," he will assume—and there will be little you will be able to do to dissuade him—that the victim is the one who came to you. We've found it effective to respond by saying (when plausible and possible) that a staff member witnessed it or heard about it. (And if possible and your acting skills are up to the challenge, instead of giving an actual name, you might even feign trying to remember the staff member's name.)

Typically you'll find that if the bully does admit to the behavior, he will respond by saying something like, "It's not a big deal—we were just joking around" or "It's okay—we're friends." Although this is merely an excuse, he might actually believe it. In our experience, the best way to handle this is to ask the bully to explain where the joke is, to ask him to explain how it was humorous, and to try to invoke a sense of empathy. In the cases where the bully claims friendship with the victim, we've feigned surprise and asked when the last time was that they hung out together outside school and if the victim would be able to corroborate the bully's claim. In most instances, the bully will understand what you're implying and that what he claimed was innocent fun is anything but that. If he is still adamant that what he was doing was a joke and you're unable to convince him otherwise, then you need to state firmly the school's position and that he needs to cease immediately; a failure to do so would be defiance on his part for which there would certainly be (additional) consequences. It is especially important to mention consequences when you meet with bullies because they generally don't realize that what to them is harmless fun and entertainment could actually result in legal action and have far-reaching effects.

But perhaps the most effective strategy for working with bullies is to remember to see them as students in need of help. It's easy to view them simply as perpetrators of offensive and hurtful actions, but it is important for you to see your interactions with them as teaching opportunities, because there is an obvious deficit in learning some lessons. Boynton and Boynton (2005) aptly remind us that it is critical to "develop good relationships with them and be a good role model for them. Positive relationships with students and adults are often lacking in a bully's life. . . . The point is that they need your attention and relationship probably more than do other students" (p. 165).

Talking with the Bully's Parents   As difficult as it is to tell parents that their child has been bullied, it is equally uncomfortable to tell parents that their child is a bully. Most parents are mortified when they hear of the kind of behavior their child has been engaging in, but as we briefly mentioned earlier, some parents can be very defensive and protective, which makes the conversation that much more difficult. In some instances, parents feel threatened because they perceive the accusation as an indictment of their parenting or child-rearing abilities. Boynton and Boynton (2005) draw on Olweus's identification of "four parenting practices that can lead to the creation of bullies: the emotional attitude of the parents, a permissive parenting attitude, physical discipline and emotional outbursts by the parents, and the temperament of the child" (p. 161), so although it is not your function to evaluate their parenting skills, through your interactions with the parents you might be able to determine whether they have created or reinforced the behavior in question. Regardless of the nature of the call or the severity of the bullying, the parents and student must know that the student is still valued by you and the school.

Implementing Schoolwide Approaches   Experts cannot seem to agree on what programs to implement schoolwide or on the efficacy of programs. One-time events—antibullying inoculations, if you will—do not seem adequate. These moments in time are not sufficient to change a school's climate and culture or to have a significant impact on bullying. On the other end of the spectrum, Rodkin (2011) cites findings by Farrington and Ttofi (2009) that "interventions that involve peers, such as using students as peer mediators or engaging bystanders to disapprove of bullying and support victims of harassment, were associated with *increases* in victimization" (p. 14). As you can see then, creating a bully-free and safe environment is certainly complex and fraught with challenges.

What seems to be clear, though, is that the culture of the school needs to be one where bullying is not tolerated. Such a culture can be developed through classroom lessons, seminars, and creating an environment where students feel safe to confide in staff members. Providing professional development to your teachers about bullying and bullying prevention as well as on how to teach schoolwide expectations can also help you reduce bullying in your school. You should also encourage your teachers to be present in the halls during class changes, especially in areas that seem to make bullying easier (stairwells, blind corners, and so on); their presence minimizes the opportunity for bullying to occur, shows students that staff are involved, and allows students to quickly find an adult if a situation occurs.

Responding to Cyberbullying

The high-profile cyberbullying cases we mentioned earlier, which were indeed horrific, caused a visceral public reaction, and such incidents lead to entreaties for immediate consequences and action whenever one occurs, including demands that the school become involved. This knee-jerk thinking is understandable, but consider for a moment the commonsense wisdom of some educators: would you (the school) get involved if you heard that over the weekend Mary said something mean about Sally while at the mall? Most likely, you would never investigate what had happened, and, even more likely, you probably wouldn't have been told about it. But because these conflicts are occurring in cyberspace and are available for parental consumption in many instances, you are more likely to receive a phone call about them. However, although there are times when you do need to become involved, which we will address shortly, your role is not to supervise the Internet and what occurs there, a truth that is sometimes difficult to tell parents and equally difficult for them to hear. In some instances, you would even be overstepping your bounds by taking any kind of action, in terms of students' right of freedom of speech and expression.

When You Can Respond to Cyberbullying   Although we encourage you to check with your district leadership or legal counsel, you should really become involved in a cyberbullying incident only when there is a nexus, or a direct connection, between something occurring in the school community and an incident taking place off of school grounds. If you have evidence of any of the following, though, you should take action to varying degrees within your capacity as an administrator:

- A threat has been made. (The legal ramifications or the violation of FCC rules would probably allow you to act.)

- There is a substantial disruption to the learning environment (although this is not always easy to prove, and you probably would not be supported if you predicted that there would be one).

- Child pornography is involved. Students don't always recognize it as such. (Confiscate the evidence, make your supervisor aware of it immediately, and turn it over to the police; you should also contact Child Protective Services.)
- The offenses are occurring during the school day (in that you have evidence that the school's equipment or Internet access are being used to enact the cyberbullying).

If you are presented with evidence of harassing text messages, obscene e-mails, phony social networking profiles, blackmail, or anything else that is either illegal or does not sit well with parents yet does not have a direct connection to the school other than students' being implicated, your response is very simple: "Although I wish I could be of more assistance, this is outside my authority, so I encourage you to contact law enforcement or the moderators of that site (or both)."

Teaching About Cyberbullying   When it comes to cyberbullying, an effective and proactive move on your part would be to provide training and classes about cyberbullying. These could take the form of professional development for your faculty during an in-service day or a faculty meeting where there is also a focus on monitoring computer usage in the classroom and the computer lab; an evening session for parents with guest speakers from local law enforcement who could also address Internet safety and online predators; and regular discussions and lessons with students during their classes.

RESOLVE STUDENT-TEACHER CONFLICTS

Conflicts are bound to occur in the classroom. No matter how skillful the teacher or how mature the student, as humans we are always susceptible to personality conflicts. In some cases, the conflict manifests itself through misbehavior (which we address in the next chapter); in other cases, the conflict is simply a matter of the teacher and student not getting along or of the student not responding to the teacher for any number of reasons. It is also natural for some students to feel that a teacher just rubs them the wrong way (and vice versa), so you can be sure that at some point you will have to address a conflict between one of your students and one of your teachers. You will need to strike a delicate balance, ensuring both that your teacher leaves feeling supported and that your student is assured that you believe in him or her. The following are some questions to ask your teacher if he or she comes to you with such a conflict:

- Have you had a one-on-one discussion with the student?

- Have you solicited help from the parents?

- Have you had a meeting with the student's counselor? Have you met with the counselor with the student present?

- Have you talked with other teachers to see if they are experiencing the same conflict? Why or why haven't they had the same experience?

- Have you talked with your department chair to ask how he or she would work with this issue?

- Have you employed strategies to get know the student outside your curriculum or class?

If the teacher has explored these options without any noticeable improvement, then you will need to facilitate a conversation between the student and the teacher. Prior to having such a meeting, it would be helpful for you and the teacher to plan how you will conduct the meeting (which could function very similarly to the student mediation process we identified earlier in the chapter) and what you are hoping for in terms of an outcome. If after the conference there are still conflicts present, you might be tempted to remove the student from the class or make a schedule change. We are hesitant to recommend this course of action except in severe instances, because once you employ this strategy, you will be increasingly pressed by teachers, students, and parents to make other schedule changes, thus introducing instability to your master schedule and classes.

The importance of a positive learning environment and school climate cannot be overstated in terms of their power to influence student achievement and student and staff morale. But even in highly effective schools, "The frequency of conflicts among students and the increasing severity of violence that characterizes such conflicts make their management costly in terms of time, energy, and money. To make schools orderly and peaceful places where high-quality instruction can take place, conflicts must be managed constructively" (Johnson and Johnson,

1995, p. 111). You will need to address and resolve these conflicts—whether they entail bullying, cyberbullying, or conflicts between friends or between students and teachers—in order to prevent further disruption to the learning environment. Although the suggestions we have presented from our experiences are certainly helpful, they are by no means an exhaustive list of how you can address conflicts in your school. We are confident that the more involved you become in handling these conflicts, the more thoroughly you will develop your techniques and strategies to complement those contained in this chapter and better assist students in learning how to cope with and address difficult situations.

Understanding and Preventing Student Misbehavior

*A*s you are about to enter your office, you pause outside your door because something has caught your eye: a wad of paper is on the verge of cascading out of your inbox. You grab the pile and slump into your chair. How is it there are so many referrals in your box when you had just emptied it two days ago and had addressed nearly all of them?

You quickly flip through them, and as expected, they cover a range of infractions: tardies, skipping, misbehavior, defiance, even theft. Staring at them, you can't help but marvel at how quiet the first month of school had been; you were able to visit classrooms, answer e-mail at a leisurely pace, and work on school and county initiatives. Now you find yourself responding to e-mail from home, postponing observations, and worrying how you will find the time to complete your work on those initiatives.

You scan your referrals again just to be sure there wasn't something you missed, and you realize that you're going to have to address some of these today. A case of theft, a student refusing to go to the main office when he was told to, and a student cursing at a teacher are all referrals that take priority. You certainly don't want any leads on the theft to go cold, and you certainly don't want your students thinking that it's okay for them to ignore directions or be disrespectful to your teachers—you simply can't have a school operate that way (not to mention that you would lose respect from both your teachers and students if you didn't address either situation in a timely fashion). The other referrals can wait, so you begin filling out passes to send for the students named in these referrals you just flagged, but quickly realize that you will probably be able to see only one student right now: your lunch duty is *coming up shortly, and the other administrators can't cover for you because they are in observations. You quickly calculate that if you eat lunch between lunch shifts, you could probably see another student before you attend a subject team meeting. Assuming that the teachers keep to their agenda that they sent you last week, you'll probably have enough time before the end of the day to begin investigating the theft.*

Although the topic of classroom management is regularly addressed in professional literature, the issue of discipline from the administrative side rarely receives the same level of attention, especially in the form of "how to." Perhaps it is because the topic of student discipline is seen as negative and cynical while most educational literature focuses on more positive things, but to ignore the topic altogether is to deny the reality of what occurs in schools all across the nation and even the world. Even in "good" schools, violations of the student code of conduct are bound to occur. Infractions ranging from the trivial or mundane to the spectacular or bizarre will all find their way down to the main office. To ignore this reality is to disregard the unspoken truth that a school's reputation is never based solely on the quality of its teachers; rather, parents, community members, and even neighboring schools regularly discuss perceptions—real and imagined—about how orderly, safe, and smoothly running the learning environment is. As Boynton and Boynton (2005), drawing on *Classroom Management That Works* (Marzano, Marzano, and Pickering, 2003), explain, "Nothing affects a building's reputation more than the level of discipline that permeates the classrooms and overall school. No staff member wants to work in a classroom or building that is chaotic or out of control. Excellent teachers request transfers from these buildings, and parents attempt to move their students out of these schools. Soon there is a vicious cycle of staff exodus, parental complaints and declining test scores" (p. v). Therefore, you have a great responsibility resting on your shoulders: to deal effectively with student discipline and ensure that there is systemic support for handling misbehavior.

As an administrator, you are probably like most others: surprised by the number of discipline issues you must address. As an effective classroom teacher, you rarely sent students to the main office or wrote referrals. Whether you worried about your administrator seeing too many referrals from you or perhaps just didn't want to undermine your own authority, you assumed that all teachers were like you: caretakers of orderly learning environments. But as an administrator you quickly learned that you were mistaken, and were astonished by what constitutes a referral to the main office, as it sometimes seems as though you are being asked to manage your teachers' classrooms for them.

DISCUSS DISCIPLINE WITH YOUR STAFF

Crucial to being an effective administrator is being an effective communicator with your staff; discussing classroom management and discipline with your staff is a part of that. First of all, "effective school discipline results from collaboratively developed, clearly stated, widely distributed and discussed school policies and procedures for both students and staff" (Simpson, 2000, p. 94). By discussing the causes of student misbehavior, ways to prevent it, and your expectations regarding discipline, you can improve the climate and discipline in your building. In addition, you need to engage your staff in soliciting their expectations of you when a student is sent to the office. Without this two-way conversation, you are likely neither to learn of nor to fulfill their expectations of you as an administrator. Furthermore, if you don't engage in these kinds of dialogues, you run the risk of fomenting confusion, frustration, and alienation among your staff. In our experience, many teachers are distrustful of administration, skeptical and cynical about what happens when you deal with students behind the closed door. Whether it is because they don't grasp the big picture, are seeking some form of divine justice for the infraction, or have been burned in the past by an administrator's dealings with discipline, some teachers believe that "nothing happens" when a student is referred to the office. These feelings, compounded by teachers' sense of helplessness and powerlessness, can undermine your authority and credibility, so it is critical that you have open and honest dialogues about student misbehavior and discipline with your teachers.

You also must engage in these conversations with teachers because although it might be hard to believe, there are some teachers who think it is their job only to teach, not to monitor student behavior. Simpson (2000) states that you should "in-service all staff and solicit the support of each staff member for policies and procedures. Stress that unanimous support will make the policies most effective and that each teacher has a professional responsibility to respond professionally to situations involving discipline" (p. 94).

Understanding Classroom Misbehavior

The reasons for classroom misbehavior are varied, and sometimes, as distressing as it sounds, you may never fully discover the reason for it. But if you share what you do know about the reasons behind classroom misbehavior with your teachers, you will certainly be helping them combat future occurrences. The following are some of the more common reasons for misbehavior in classrooms.

Lack of Skills　There is research that claims that students misbehave not because they lack motivation or the basic academic skills to succeed (although these can be contributing factors) but because, as Greene (2010, p. 29) puts it, "they lack the skills *not* to be challenging." As Greene explains, "the skills they lack include crucial cognitive skills, especially in the domains of flexibility/adaptability, frustration tolerance, and problem solving" (p. 29). He argues that "if they had these skills, they'd use them—because they'd prefer *not* to be behaviorally challenging. That's because doing well is preferable to not doing well" (p. 29). Although the extent of this problem is debatable, lack of these skills can certainly be a reason for a student's misbehavior.

Work Avoidance　Many students act out as a way of avoiding the assigned work or task at hand. Although there are times when it is simply because a student does not feel like doing any work, in many cases it is because he or she lacks the necessary skills and does not want others to realize this. Similarly, a student's low self-esteem can also cause him to misbehave in class; doing so is his way of improving his sense of worth as well as what he believes to be his stature in the eyes of his peers. Thus misbehavior functions as a type of survival skill, a technique designed to help him avoid doing what is asked of him.

Boredom　Some students are simply bored being in class or by the subject matter. With so many other high-tech options for entertainment, sitting still for sometimes ninety minutes at a time causes students to disconnect and seek other forms of entertainment, mainly acting out. And even if they are interested in the subject matter, the presentation or style of delivery may turn them off or doesn't allow them to be engaged, so they divert their attention and energy elsewhere.

Drug or Alcohol Abuse　Many students who have substance abuse issues find it difficult to pass the day without using, and this difficulty manifests itself in their classroom behavior. They can appear agitated and are quick to snap at others. Some might even desire to be sent out of the room in order to find a way to satisfy their needs.

Alienation   Although feelings of alienation are common during adolescence, there are some students whose sense of alienation or disenfranchisement is so profound that they negatively react to the overall school structure, their classes, and even socially accepted norms. As a result of these feelings, they are often oppositional and nonconforming to anything "mainstream," which includes classroom rules.

Attention   Students, especially adolescents, seem to be on a constant quest for attention—either positive or negative—for a variety of reasons. It might be that they are seeking the attention they believe they lack at home or depend on from their peers. Regardless of the reason, they will misbehave because they crave being the center of attention in class.

Credibility   For some students, acting in a negative manner, such as by disrupting instruction or disrespecting teachers, is a way for them to earn credibility and respect with some of their peers. This is seen particularly in students who feel that it is more important to be seen as "bad" or who want to cultivate a negative reputation rather than be recognized for positive behaviors and accomplishments.

Home Life   Many students act out—consciously or unconsciously—because of what might be occurring in their homes. The sadness, confusion, frustration, or pain caused by their family dynamic and personal situations can often manifest itself in misbehavior. In these cases, misbehavior is not so much a problem as it is a symptom.

Entitlement   If you ask any adult today, he or she is likely to tell you that, unlike even a decade ago, these days students seem to be acting out of a sense of entitlement. Among other causes, our instant gratification society may have something to do with this kind of behavior, but you might also find that it is reinforced at home.

Lack of Boundaries   Teachers who do not create or enforce firm classroom rules or who establish loose boundaries in an attempt to befriend students often have discipline problems in their classes. Students overstep boundaries because they don't know where the line is or because the line shifts; then the teacher is suddenly frustrated (much to the student's surprise) by behavior that had previously seemed acceptable.

Personality Conflict   The fact of the matter is, students won't like all of their teachers. A student who has never previously been in trouble might suddenly be bumping heads with one of his teachers for no other apparent reason than "because I don't like him."

Because They Can   Many students misbehave quite simply because they *can*. Some figure out what their teachers' "buttons" are and enjoy the free entertainment that comes with pushing them. Still others act out because the class lacks structure, routine, authority, or engaging lessons.

Neither you nor the classroom teacher has control over all of these various causes for classroom misbehavior. (For more information on misbehavior and classroom management, we encourage you to refer to *Discipline with Dignity* [Curwin, Mendler, and Mendler, 2008]). However, there are some strategies that you can share with your teachers to assist them in handling misbehavior, which will also lighten the load of discipline that you will have to address, as we explain in the next section.

Minimizing Student Misbehavior

Student misbehavior—actions and behaviors that are contrary in varying degrees to acceptable conduct—is bound to occur because we are dealing with human nature; what matters, though, is how teachers react and respond to the infractions in their classroom. For many teachers, an office referral is their first (and only) line of defense; however, referrals "should only be used for the most serious and visible issues" (Boynton and Boynton, 2005, p. 68). Therefore, to preserve the efficacy of an office referral, encourage your teachers to use them as a last resort and then provide some professional development to support their efforts in classroom management, discipline, and instruction.

The first step you need to take to minimize classroom misbehavior is to share with your teachers your expectations regarding how it should be addressed. (This is also a good time to hear their expectations of you in regard to discipline.) You should convey to your teachers that it is critical that they try to handle the infractions (of course not the major ones) that occur in their classes. Doing so will bolster their authority and credibility with their students. You need to explain that although you can certainly give consequences to the student, if the teacher is unwilling or unable to deal with misbehavior himself or herself, by stepping in you are ultimately undermining the teacher's authority, and the message that will unconsciously and unintentionally be sent to the class is that the teacher is neither in control nor in charge. This in turn will result in a bigger and messier classroom management problem for him or her in the future.

Another important piece in preventing, or at least minimizing, student misbehavior is to develop a schoolwide and proactive approach to it. For example, you should stress to your teachers the importance of establishing clear expectations with their students. These expectations, policies, practices, and consequences could be developed as a faculty so that they are consistent in all areas of the building. You should also engage your teachers in a discussion about schoolwide rules (are they clear, visible, and supported?) as well as about the continuum of responses to infractions. Marzano, Marzano, and Pickering (2003) suggest holding "an open house night for parents who have questions about the schoolwide rules and procedures" and providing "students and parents with a written copy of those rules and procedures" (p. 109).

A more specific example of a schoolwide approach to student behavior can be seen in how some schools have come to the conclusion that if they expect good behavior from their students, then they need to describe what that looks like and teach it to their students. This mentality generally manifests itself in such programs as PBIS, which stands for Positive Behavioral Interventions and Supports and is used interchangeably with Schoolwide Positive Behavior Supports. PBIS is "based on principles of applied behavior analysis and the prevention approach and values of positive support" (http://pbis.org/pbis_faq.aspx). It is a framework or approach for teaching students appropriate behavior and addressing classroom management and disciplinary issues. In a PBIS school, there is a focus "on three to five behavioral expectations that are positively stated and easy to remember. In other words, rather than telling students what not to do, the school will focus on the preferred behaviors" (http://pbis.org/school/swpbs_for_beginners.aspx). Staff members then agree on common expectations, language, and responses to student misbehavior, and the positive behavior is emphasized over exclusionary consequences through some kind of reward program.

The next piece of staff development for your teachers is to offer them strategies to help maintain an orderly learning environment. Doing so helps you "proactively solve potential problems so that the office referral system is strong and effective" (Boynton and Boynton, 2005, p. 69), so that when you do receive a referral, you will know it is for a serious issue and that your teachers will have tried various other interventions before referring the student. The following are some brief tips and techniques you might consider sharing with your teachers:

Develop Engaging Lessons   Perhaps this first tip seems a bit obvious, but we'd be remiss if we didn't mention the power of an engaging, stimulating lesson that offers a variety of choices and activities that appeal to multiple intelligences. Although such lessons won't eliminate student misbehavior, they certainly do minimize it: students have little opportunity to participate in off-task behavior when they are engaged in the task at hand. So use this opportunity to discuss student motivation and engagement with your staff, perhaps even referencing such works as *Instruction for All Students* (Rutherford, 2002) or *The Highly Engaged Classroom* (Marzano and Pickering, with Heflebower, 2010) as an entry point for staff development on sound instructional practices that can also help minimize student misbehavior.

Establish Clear Procedures and Routines   How a class functions (how assignments are turned in, how work is returned to students, how missing work is communicated, how attendance is taken, how materials are distributed or collected, how students are able to leave the room, how students ask for assistance, and so forth) can have an impact on student behavior. A poorly organized classroom (and lesson) or inconsistent procedures create downtime (and sometimes chaos) in the midst of which students are more likely to misbehave. Establishing, teaching, and reinforcing procedures and routines early in the school year can help minimize off-task behaviors.

Employ Proximity and Mobility   When teachers exercise mobility in their classroom, students have less opportunity to engage in off-task behavior, especially when they don't know where their teacher is moving to next in the room. Help novices and veterans alike understand that sometimes all it takes to get a student back on track is simply to stand near him or to lightly touch or tap his desk. Aside from the issue of behavior monitoring, teachers who barricade themselves behind a desk or podium seriously hinder their ability to forge a connection with students, and such a connection is an even more valuable tool to help with classroom management.

Practice "Withitness" The most effective teachers are those who have the skill known as "withitness." Marzano, Marzano, and Pickering (2003), drawing on Jacob Kounin, who coined the term, state that it is a "disposition of the teacher to quickly and accurately identify problem behavior or potential problem behavior and to act on it immediately" (p. 67). The teachers who possess this skill convey to their students that they have eyes in the back of their head, so to speak, and are aware of what is occurring in all areas among all students in the classroom.

Develop Class Rules All teachers establish some form of expressed rules of behavior in their classes, but many teachers don't develop these rules in cooperation with their students or base them on a discussion about values. Doing so helps create buy-in for students and crystallizes expectations. Most teachers are familiar with the idea that the fewer the rules, the better, but you might want not only to stress to your teachers that specific rules are more desirable but also, as Curwin, Mendler, and Mendler (2008) explain, to encourage them to frame the rules using positive language—for example, "Please come to class on time" rather than "Don't be late."

Build Rapport Building rapport with students is an essential way for your teachers to better manage their classrooms. Many teachers understand this, but some of them view conversations with their students about the subject matter and how they are faring academically as evidence of relationship building. Instead, encourage your teachers to "build relationships deliberately," as Bondy and Ross (2008, p. 54) explain. Offer your teachers ways to develop rapport with their students through discussions about their likes and dislikes, interests, involvement in extracurricular activities, and other such topics, demonstrating care about the students as people, not just as a set of test scores. In our experience, teachers who survey their students about their likes and interests when school begins find it easier to maintain their students' attention; however, Bondy and Ross note that this technique will work only if students believe the teacher's interest to be sincere, and if the teacher actually makes use of the information. Savvy teachers find ways to incorporate this information into their lesson plans in both subtle and overt ways. But your teachers should always keep in mind that "Day-to-day interactions are more important than formal questionnaires. A smile, a hand on the shoulder, the use of a student's name, a question that shows you remember something the student has mentioned—these small gestures do much to develop relationships. Don't underestimate their power" (p. 56).

In cases where your teachers might offer push-back about building rapport because they have some difficult students, you might recommend that they try the "two-by-ten strategy," described by Smith and Lambert (2008). These authors note that "the students who seemingly deserve the most punitive consequences we can muster are actually the ones who most need a positive personal connection with their teacher. When they act out, they are letting us know that they are seeking a positive connection with an adult authority figure and that they need that connection first, before they can focus on learning content" (p. 19). In this strategy, which Smith and Lambert attribute to the work of Raymond Wlodkowski (1983), your teacher would for two minutes a day for ten days in a row have a personal—yet appropriate—conversation with their most challenging student. In a finding supported by Wlodkowski's research, Smith and Lambert found that behavior improved, and teachers found "an ally in the class" (p. 19).

Don't Ignore the Behavior   Some teachers mistakenly believe that if they ignore the behavior, the problem will ultimately correct and resolve itself. Although we certainly don't mean to imply that your teachers need to be hawks in their classrooms, we do suggest that if the offending behavior is blatant, ignoring it is ultimately consenting to it. Teachers need to inform parents when the problem is obvious and while it is still manageable.

Call Home   A phone call to a parent usually has a more powerful impact on the student than a referral to the office. As obvious as the benefits of calling home may seem, you will find that many teachers underutilize this option. You might encourage your teachers to call home early in the year to introduce themselves to their students' parents as a way to build rapport with them. One of the greatest mistakes your teachers will probably make if they do call home is waiting too long to do so; urge them to call home early and often rather than waiting until midway through the year when they are frustrated, which only frustrates parents, who will wish they had known earlier that there was a problem. Provide current contact numbers to your teachers and encourage them to keep a communication log documenting their attempts to speak with parents as well as actual conversations.

Move Seats   This is an oldie but a goodie. Show your teachers how to strategically place troublesome or talkative students in the classroom rather than merely relegating them to the back row; suggest different room setups to ease mobility. You might also discuss with them the advantages (and disadvantages) of creating a quarterly seating chart.

Master "the Look"   It is not an easy skill to acquire, but giving "the look" is a critical technique familiar to experienced teachers; it is essential that you share this trade secret with your novice teachers to help them minimize classroom misbehavior. Boynton and Boynton (2005) describe this technique as "looking intently at a student who is beginning to get off task . . . [to] draw his or her attention back to the matter at hand. This type of look communicates that you are aware of what the student is doing and that you wish the undesirable behavior to stop" (p. 38). "The look" will help your teachers maintain their students' respect.

Observe Other Teachers   A great way for your teachers to expand their repertoire of classroom management strategies is for them to observe other teachers in action. (We discuss this further in Chapter Eight.) If you offer this possibility to your teachers, then be sure to take an active role in making it happen by selecting the teacher to be observed, setting up the observation, and arranging for class coverage if necessary. Be sure to follow up with your teacher to discuss what he observed and how he thinks he can incorporate it in his own classroom.

Use Silence   Having your teachers simply be quiet rather than talking or shouting over their students can be a powerful tool for helping them manage their classrooms. Although silence is especially effective in elementary settings, it can also be useful in a secondary setting if it is not abused.

Never Use Sarcasm   Even though teachers might think that their students are savvy enough to understand sarcasm, they run the risk of hurting and humiliating them by using sarcasm in the classroom, especially as a management technique. Although humor can be effective, sarcasm can escalate a situation.

Increase Praise   Everyone likes to be praised for doing something well or doing something right; students are no different. If your teachers do not offer their students genuine praise, they run the risk of creating a negative classroom environment, which can lend itself to misbehavior. Students generally want to work for someone's praise, so encourage your teachers to praise their students' efforts and attempts as well as their answers and questions.

Talk in Private   For many teachers, their gut reaction is to immediately reprimand a student in front of the class, to make an example of him in hopes of deterring future misbehavior. It is your responsibility to explain to your teachers the pitfalls of publicly reprimanding their students: that these kinds of confrontations are rarely effective in the long run and ultimately escalate the situation, as the student will likely try to save face among his peers. So instead encourage your teachers to pull students aside during a transition or when they are engaged in a task. Also encourage your teachers to speak with the student after class and to hold conferences with the student, her parents, and the guidance counselor.

Give Consequences   As long as your teachers contact their students' parents, there should be nothing preventing them from giving their students their own reasonable consequences. Help them brainstorm possibilities, such as after-school or lunch detention or some kind of service activity to which the parents consent. Stress to your teachers that they must inform parents if they plan on keeping students after school.

Create Rewards   We've known many teachers who have implemented some type of reward system in their classes to reinforce positive behavior and discourage inappropriate behavior. Students either receive tangible rewards or tokens that they can accumulate and exchange for privileges, such as a homework pass, or activities, such as a pizza party. Some teachers devise their system so that students can also *lose* credit they have earned.

Model What You Value   Too many educators fall prey to the "because I am an adult" mentality. For example, if cell phone use is not permitted in the building, teachers will vigorously enforce this rule, but some will then use their cell phones in the hall, at lunch, and so on. Help your teachers understand that they need to model what they value. If they adopt this kind of double standard, students will dub them hypocrites or phonies and lose respect for them, which can lead to (more) misbehavior in class.

Although this is not an exhaustive list of techniques, it does give you a starting point for how you can help your teachers. What is important to keep in mind is that the "guiding principle for disciplinary interventions is that they should include a healthy balance between negative consequences for inappropriate behavior and positive consequences for appropriate behavior" (Marzano, Marzano, and Pickering, 2003, p. 40).

REVIEW DISCIPLINE DATA

In addition to understanding some of the causes of student misbehavior and helping your teachers minimize it, another important strategy for you to employ as an administrator is to get a global picture of the misbehavior and disciplinary infractions in your building by tracking and reviewing your school's discipline data. Many schools have student information management systems that will produce these data; if yours does not, it is not difficult to create a spreadsheet or a database to help you accomplish the same thing. In analyzing your student discipline, you should consider the following questions:

- Is there a particular area in the building where more infractions tend to occur?
- Is there a certain time of day that yield more or fewer referrals?
- What is the average number of referrals per teacher?
- Which teachers exceed that average?
- What is the percentage of disciplinary referrals for male students versus female students?
- What is the percentage of disciplinary referrals by ethnicity?
- Are there significant discrepancies between genders or among students of different ethnicities?
- What is the percentage of referrals for special education students?
- Are there certain classes that have a higher number of referrals?

- Are we seeing an increase or decrease in discipline referrals compared to previous years?
- How does our discipline record compare to similar schools in the district?

For each of these questions, you should also be prepared to ask "Why?" in order to help you to get to the root of whatever is occurring. Examining the answers to these kinds of questions can ultimately help you reduce the number of student discipline referrals. For example, if you determine a pattern of incidents in a specific hallway during a class change, you might discover that there are several teachers off during that period who are consequently leaving the area once class ends and therefore are not in the halls helping monitor the transition. The same might be true if there were problems in an area of the building during a certain class time; then you know that you need to allocate your resources differently—for example, by stationing teachers or making yourself more visible near the "hot spot." A large number of infractions during a particular lunch shift might indicate the need for more cafeteria monitors or the need to reduce the number of students on that lunch shift. And most important, if you were to see a pattern of referrals from a specific teacher, you then have data and an entry point for having a dialogue with him about what is (or is not) occurring in his classroom.

MAKE CONNECTIONS

Before we can explore strategies for addressing discipline, it's important to briefly address the value of making connections with your students. Discipline, at all levels within the school, has the potential to overwhelm you, so it is essential to keep in mind that even if you are spending 80 percent of your time dealing with discipline, the students you see probably make up only 20 percent of the population (if that)—meaning that the vast majority of your students are neither troublemakers nor habitual offenders. Most students will thus never be in your office on a regular basis because they never get in trouble. Consider how depressing it would be for you never to meet any of these students, allowing the other 20 percent to monopolize your time! If you don't get out of the main office and make connections with other students, you will quickly learn that "doing discipline" can have a vampiric quality: it will suck the life out of you, as some administrators like to say. Interacting with only that small segment of the population will drain you, and you will eventually come to resent your job, your students, and possibly even yourself. You should therefore make it a point every day to set aside some time to interact with other members of the student population as well as with your "frequent flyers" in a nondisciplinary setting.

Making connections with students is also important so that they can see you as someone other than just some administrator in the main office they've heard about who knows the names of all the "bad students"—but no one else's. And if any of these students end up in your office for discipline, your job will be a little bit easier because you made a connection with them and they have seen you in a different light. The same holds true for your "regular customers" as well; if they see you taking an interest in them outside of just a disciplinary setting, many of them will come to appreciate you and realize that you are not "out to get them" and don't have it in for them. This in turn might even motivate them to stay out of your office for disciplinary reasons. Most important, seeing and interacting with these students in a different way will help you see them as real people, not just as problems or invasions of your time. Most of the techniques suggested for teachers on how to build rapport and positive relationships with students (Boynton and Boynton, 2005; McLeod, Fisher, and Hoover, 2003; Marzano, Marzano, and Pickering, 2003) are just as effective for an administrator; the following are some additional ways to help you make connections and build rapport with your students:

Use Students' Names   As an administrator, you might be responsible for hundreds of students, and as daunting as it is to learn all of their names, students will generally respect you more if you know who they are. Students understand that if you know them by name, you know them as real people, as someone's child who has worth.

Demonstrate Respect   Many students need respect before they can give respect. So pay particular attention to how you approach students both in disciplinary and social settings. Your tone and attitude can either build rapport or damage your credibility, so view every interaction as a way to demonstrate your respect for the students.

Develop Trust   Students need to know that they can trust you. Of course they also need to understand that there are certain topics that you are compelled to share, but if students feel that they can trust you with information or with their goals, you are already on your way to developing a strong rapport with them. Another way you can develop trust is by being responsive to their needs, so if you promise to look into or take care of an issue, be sure to follow up on it as soon as possible.

Share Information About Yourself   Of course you need to give consideration to what information is appropriate to share and when it is appropriate to do so, but divulging something about yourself or making yourself a little vulnerable by admitting to personal likes, dislikes, and shortcomings is a powerful way to make a connection with students.

Eat in the Cafeteria   Although it is very tempting to eat your lunch in your office to have some downtime to yourself or to catch up on work, eating in the cafeteria when students have their lunch is a great way to interact with them and to see them in a different environment.

Attend a Noncoverage Event   If you don't have administrative coverage for the night of the school play (or concert, debate, and so on), you should plan on attending it anyway to see your students excel in areas of interest to them. Moreover, you might even consider bringing your family to the event to help your students and community see you as a real person and not just a disciplinarian.

Recognize Achievements   Stay informed about which students are being recognized for their achievements and make it a point to personally commend them. Taking an active interest in their success demonstrates that you know them as more than a name on a piece of paper.

Enlist Others' Assistance   As hard as you may try to connect with a student, there will be those who remain indifferent or aloof. When that happens, it is important not to give up. In these instances, you might want to ask colleagues how they have connected with these students (Mendler, 2001).

A successful school requires successful teachers and students. Teachers' effectiveness and student achievement are diminished when teachers must spend a disproportionate amount of time dealing with misbehavior. You have an obligation to ensure a safe and positive learning environment for both your students and your staff, so preventing and resolving problems that distract from learning are among your most critical responsibilities. But even if you work with teachers on enhancing their instruction, deepening their understanding of the causes and prevention of student misbehavior, and developing appropriate relationships with their students, some students will still find their way to your office, so the next chapter focuses on ways to conduct those necessary disciplinary conversations.

Dealing with Student Discipline

*T*wo students are sitting outside your office waiting to see you as soon as Mark, another student, gets off the phone with his mother. Because you know that there are times when Mark can find speaking to his mother a little challenging, you are relieved by how supportive she is and how well the conversation goes on this occasion. You turn your attention to organizing the referrals you have for the two students outside your office waiting to see you. Meanwhile, a red-faced teacher, hand on hip, is fuming outside your door with Bryan, one of your more frequent flyers, in tow, glaring at her. As soon as Mark hangs up the phone and you write him a pass to go to class, the teacher stands directly in front of your door waiting for you to open it. Before you can even ask what is going on, she waves a referral in your face and exclaims, "I've had enough of his disrespect: I can't take it anymore! I've called his parents, I've conferenced with his family, and tried everything else, but I can't take it! He needs to see you for discipline!" To which Bryan immediately responds with a snicker as the teacher storms off, leaving you with the referral in your hand and Bryan and the other two students waiting to see what you will do next.

The word *discipline* has many meanings—you might discipline a puppy, enter a religious discipline, choose a discipline of study, or engage in a daily discipline to improve a skill. Even with all these varied meanings, it's not easy to find a definition for the word that specifically refers to dealing with students in an educational setting. Some view discipline as punishment; for others, it is a deterrent against future misbehavior. Discipline can also include rewarding and reinforcing positive or desired behaviors, but it is best understood as teaching students how to control their behavior, gaining their cooperation, and giving consequences to modify future behavior. For our purposes, when we refer to discipline, we are specifically talking about any or all of the following: receiving office referrals for student misbehavior, meeting with students because of misbehavior, and issuing consequences for violations of the school's rules and regulations.

These discipline problems "originate with students, who are young and inexperienced with respect to appropriate behaviors associated with school attendance, the use of improper language, work habits, dress, acceptance of responsibility, and self-discipline. Unlike mature adults, students lack experience in solving problems and dealing with crises. As a result, they make mistakes" (Simpson, 2000, p. 93). And in some cases, as you well know, the mistakes can even be intentional. Regardless, your responsibility is to treat each student and situation with an open mind, fairly and respectfully, and to offer empathy and sympathy when appropriate. Moreover, you should "exercise [your] responsibility to a student by consistently and persistently educating [him or her] toward more acceptable positive actions that will be beneficial to all students in a school and to the school's staff" (p. 93).

Many administrators don't relish having to "do discipline." Understandably, it can be overwhelming, it can be a negative experience, and it can even detract and distract from some of the more "prestigious" leadership activities in which they would rather engage. Nevertheless, "disciplining students is truly an instructional activity . . . [because their job] is always to do whatever [they] can to ensure that the instructional programs of students are not impeded, and classrooms with disruptions caused by misbehaving students will not be effective learning environments" (Daresh, 2004, p. 38). In this regard, you can view your handling of disciplinary tasks as a positive contribution: you are helping make your teachers' jobs a little easier and improving the quality of your school's environment.

Before we discuss the more day-to-day aspects of discipline, we want to note that it is important that you develop a philosophy with regard to student discipline and attune your responses to your school system's policies. You might confer with your supervisor about the district's view on discipline as well as its classification of offenses. For example, you need to learn your district's policies on suspension, its rules as to when you must notify or conference with parents, and its reporting requirements.

REVIEW YOUR REFERRALS

It has ceased amazing us how quickly referrals can pile up. Even when you devote an entire day to working solely on discipline, you may very well walk in the very next morning and again encounter an inbox overflowing with referrals. You may find this mound of referrals so regular or yourself stretched so thin that you only review the referrals when you are absolutely ready with the necessary time set aside to address them. Waiting to find time to address them is not wrong; what is problematic, though, is not knowing what kind of referrals you have in your box until you actually decide to work on them.

We've known administrators who have functioned this way and were then surprised and consequently embarrassed when they came across an old referral in their box that should have been addressed immediately because of the severity or immediacy of the issue. Regularly thumbing through the referrals in your box helps you be aware of issues that are brewing; you can then give highest priority to those infractions that need to be addressed immediately and in the near future, as well as determine which ones can wait. For example, it might not be as impor-tant that you talk with a student as soon as you receive a referral reporting him for cutting a class, but if you suddenly find a referral in your box about a fight, a potential fight, or a student who made a threat—especially against a staff member—you would obviously want to address it right away.

Unfortunately, we have known administrators who waited an inordinate amount of time to pull the referrals out of their box, only to be surprised to find out about a student who had hit another student in class or had even threatened physical harm to a teacher. By waiting so long to review referrals, these adminis-trators unwittingly not only appeared unresponsive but also conveyed the message to their teachers that they did not take the referrals seriously. There is nothing worse than having your teachers think that you do not support them, especially when it comes to serious infractions.

As a side note, if you do find a critical referral buried in your inbox, after you handle the incident it is also a good idea to speak with the teacher who left it in your box. These types of referrals should be hand delivered to you or to someone in the main office who will ensure that you get the referral immediately, but most teachers are not aware that administrators might not check their inbox on an hourly basis. Some might even worry that they would be bothering you with it; others might feel that even though it was a serious incident, they handled it anyway, and (incorrectly) didn't think you needed to see the student immediately. Therefore, you should explain to your teachers under what circumstances you should be contacted immediately and to let them know how they can reach you if they have that kind of referral. This is especially important because there are times when you're not in the building, so it should be clearly articulated what should be done in your absence. To begin with, identify the following for your teachers as critical incidents:

- Fights, either physical or serious verbal confrontations
- Rumors of fights
- Threats, whether they involve students, staff, or people outside school
- Possession of a weapon
- Sexual harassment or assault
- Possession of an illegal substance
- Possession of alcohol
- Possession of inappropriate material
- Possession of someone else's property
- Being under the influence of drugs or alcohol
- Self-inflicted harm or the desire to inflict such harm
- Physical or verbal abuse at home
- Gang activity

It has been our experience that not all teachers, especially novice ones, are aware of the need to immediately report knowledge of these kinds of incidents or the legal ramifications of not doing so. In terms of reporting these incidents, highlight methods to your staff that include finding another administrator, speaking with the safety and security specialist, e-mailing you in case you're in front of your computer (with the explanation that they should avoid using identifiable information that could cause the email to be released through a Freedom of Information Act request), notifying a main-office secretary to locate you, or seeking out a guidance counselor or even the school nurse.

Reviewing your referrals is equally helpful if you have students who are already on your radar. All administrators have students on whom they need to be keeping tabs, on whom they have been asked to keep tabs, or about whom they have asked teachers to notify them as soon as there is a problem. Keeping abreast of your referrals helps you avoid looking ineffective when teachers find you later and want an update on a student about whom you had originally asked them to keep you updated.

ENGAGE YOUR STUDENTS

Until you actually talk with your students in your office, you are never really sure which way the encounter will go—even with the most seemingly cut-and-dried referrals. Each student is unique, so you need to find the right approach for engaging with him or her in your office. With some, a firm approach might be the only way, whereas with others, you know you need to be a little more indirect and softer around the edges. With that in mind, we offer the following strategies and techniques to assist you in engaging your students.

Ask, "Why Are You Down Here?"

On the surface, it seems playful to ask a student this question when he or she arrives in your office. But what we generally find is that many students are suddenly embarrassed that you are asking them why you had to call them to your office to speak with them. Many of them will immediately admit to what they did or why they were referred, thereby saving you from having to question them or find a way to get them to admit a wrongdoing. But just as many students will volunteer information about an infraction (or infractions) you were unaware of, thinking that these were what you were after in the first place. They might respond, "Oh! Is this about the stolen iPod?" Meanwhile, you probably knew nothing about a stolen iPod and had instead called them down about being tardy to a class. Naturally, your response would be, "Yes, what can you tell me about the iPod?" or you could ask, "Was it an actual iPod?" At that point, you might choose to defer for the time being the reason why they were called down in the first place (though of course you will have to get back to that issue too).

Say, "Tell Me What Happened"

We almost always ask students to go first and explain what the situation was or what happened, rather than start off by telling them what we had heard. Aside from the fact that we can sometimes gain information that we might have been unaware of, this technique allows us to immediately deflate the situation. Rather than allowing the student to simmer in her chair while we tell her what the teacher said (which also immediately leads the student to believe that we are "siding with the teacher" even when we are simply relaying what we were told), our asking the student to explain the situation grants her the opportunity of an immediate release, as many students are ready to blow by the time they make it to the office. Some might argue that when working with both the teacher and the student in the office, you should permit the teacher to give his version first as a sign of respect; however, we still let the student speak first (although when possible, you might want to explain your rationale to your teacher beforehand). Further, if you make it a point to ask the student to tell you what happened as soon as you see her, you also ensure that she is being given due process.

Say, "Let's Focus on You"

It won't come as a surprise to you, but when students are called or sent to the main office for discipline, the majority of them will immediately try to take control of the situation or discussion. They will repeatedly attempt to divert the conversation to something else, anyone else, in order to take the focus off of them. Although it might seem elementary that you need to keep the focus on them and what they did, it is often difficult to do so, and even the most skilled administrators can fall prey to students' efforts to go off on verbal tangents. Trying to navigate these digressions is nearly impossible, so the best thing to do is to continually bring the focus back to the student. It might sound simple, but saying something like "Okay, but let's focus on you" is an effective way to keep bringing the conversation back to where it needs to be.

Another way that students will try to divert the focus is to use the age-old excuse that we all have used at some point in our lives: "But everyone else was doing [whatever it was] too." Students cling to this defense in the belief that they cannot be held accountable if other students were doing the same thing too. (This is like the similarly age-old rationalization, "They can't give us all detention.") The logic of this argument appears sound to students, so trying to prove to them otherwise can be frustrating. However, one method we have found to be successful, especially with high school students, is to use the metaphor of driving.

You can begin by asking if the student drives yet, and if he doesn't, you can preface the example by saying that you're sure he has seen something like this or has even been a witness to it himself. Then present a scenario in which a car is pulled over by the police for speeding on the highway. And of course, every driver's response or explanation to the policeman is, "But officer, everyone else is speeding." And we're sure that you can anticipate the officer's frustrating response: "But *you're* the one I caught." Although we realize that this scenario has the potential to elicit the "But it's not fair" response, it does seem to teach a lesson or at least get the student to understand that he has a measure of culpability in whatever had happened that caused him to be sent to the main office.

Another effective response for when students claim that others were doing the same thing that they are being accused of is to explain the possible reasons why they were the one singled out. For example, you could decide to play on the idea of leadership. Ask the student the following: "Do you think it is possible that the teacher singled you out because she thought that if you were to behave, then maybe the rest would as well because you are so popular [so well liked, such a leader]?" Using this tactic can give your student a glimpse into the inner workings of teachers' decision making as well as the bigger picture, which is their classroom environment.

Say, "You Made a Poor Choice"

Another effective way to keep the focus on what the student did is to separate the student from the choice. We've found that taking this tack is helpful for dealing with both students and their parents: no parent wants to think that their child is a bad person, and most students appreciate not being seen a certain way or cast in a particular light.

You might say something along the lines of "I don't think you are a bad person, but I do think you made a bad choice" or "What you did doesn't make you a bad person, but it was a poor choice, and how you handle yourself in the aftermath of that choice is what will define you." You should definitely stress the idea of how we grow from mistakes, oftentimes learning more from our failures than from our successes.

You can also substitute the word "behavior" for "choice" for the same effect. Stress to the student that you and her teacher don't dislike her as a person, rather that it is her behavior that you find offensive or unacceptable. By using that kind of language, you are not beating up on the student's self-esteem and are instead helping her preserve some of her dignity. Further, by using these kinds of words, you are suggesting that the student can be in control if she chooses to be—she can control her behaviors, her choices, and her future actions, whereas she might not feel that she can control who she is as a person (for example, her background, her life, and so on). Similarly, for the student who feels remorse for what she has done, you can help her focus not on her past actions but on her future behaviors and choices. Help her understand that even though she might be beating herself up over her past actions, it is only her future actions that she has control over.

It is also helpful to point out to students that their infractions were usually avoidable, that they are in your office for a *choice* they made. We do realize that this in and of itself does not normally correct the behavior; instead, what we are attempting to do is correct the mentality. The notion of "I couldn't help it" or "It's not my fault" seems to be so prevalent today that it is important to illustrate to students that they are making conscious choices and that they have the power to change their actions.

Ask, "What Will You Do Differently?"

In helping students change their behavior and avoid future consequences, you need to help them understand more fully the concept of choices (and by extension, alternatives) and their consequences. As Daresh (2004) points out, "It is worthwhile remembering that discipline is best understood not as punishment, but rather as a form of counseling and student advisement" (p. 38). Let's suppose that a student is in your office because he was involved in a fight. After the student explains why he got in the fight, it would behoove you to ask the student, "What could you have done differently?" Remarkably, many students are unable (or don't want) to identify what they could have done to avoid getting entangled in the situation they suddenly found themselves in. Help your students recognize how they could have avoided getting in trouble, such as by walking away, ignoring the other student(s), declining to escalate the situation, calling out for help, getting a teacher, or reporting the instigating action to you. As an adult, you might assume that these kinds of choices are obvious, but adolescents are ruled by passions and peer pressures and as a result are sometimes not able to think clearly.

As important as it is to focus on what the student could have done differently and on alternatives to the choice he made, it is equally important to end the conversation with what he *will* do differently in the future. Although the options will most likely be the same, what is important is getting a commitment from the student about what he will do differently. Because the word "try" is so prevalent in youth culture ("I'm not trying to fail that class," "I'm not trying to have problems," "I'm not trying to have drama in my life," and so on), we sometimes use the following example to stress a point with them about "trying." We place a pencil on a table in front of the student, delineate an area of about a square foot, and say, "Try to move the pencil outside the square foot." Students will immediately pick up the pencil and move it outside the area, at which point we instruct them to put it back down. We repeat the direction again, emphasizing the key word more this time: "*Try* to move the pencil." Many students will quickly realize that we are playing with words, but it is an important exercise: when students repeatedly use the word "try," it becomes an escape hatch for them—it releases them from the possibility of succeeding, of failing, of responsibility. It excuses them from engaging in any real attempt to do anything differently next time. And so along those lines, we quote the famous words of Yoda from the *Star Wars* trilogy: "Try not. Do or do not. There is no try."

It is important that students understand the potential for future consequences. Although it is helpful for them to brainstorm what they can do differently in the future if they are in the same situation again, given human nature and the fact that they are children, there still remains a good chance that they will make the same mistake again. By stating what will happen if they again make a poor choice, you are presenting them with a deterrent and, you hope, a reminder that will pop in their head at just the right time. Further, if they do end up in your office again, you immediately have an opening with them: "What did I say [or what did we agree on] would happen if this occurred again?" You can thus eliminate complaints about consequences and save yourself the stress of having an argument over the need for consequences. It eliminates the "surprise factor," meaning that students are less likely to say, "Well, I didn't know this was going to happen!" because you can respond, "Remember when we talked last month and I explained that this would be your consequence if this behavior continued?" If you keep a record of your student conferences, you could even pull out your notes and share them. This kind of recollection, reference, and warning is just as useful when talking with your student's parents.

Say, "Tell Your Mom What You Did"

Sometimes an effective way to prevent future misbehavior is to have students explain their present infraction to their parents. Students sometimes seem comfortable with their misbehavior because they can simply sit back in a chair while you explain the situation to their parents on the phone; in many instances, they even get to put their own spin on it once they arrive home from school. After we have addressed the referral and given consequences, we have found it effective to call the parent and hand the phone to the student, telling him, "Tell your mom what happened" or "Explain to your dad why you are in my office." It is easy for a student to have *you* explain to his parents the obscene language he used in class, or to explain when he gets home that it was a misunderstanding and that he hadn't actually done anything; it is difficult for a student to wiggle out of telling a parent on the phone in your office what actually occurred, especially with you sitting across from him correcting and prompting as needed.

Many students balk at the idea, but we are quick to explain, "Why should we be the ones to tell them? We didn't do anything wrong!" And if a parent is actually on the line while you are holding the phone out to him, most students will not leave their parent hanging like that. If they do refuse to take the phone, be sure to explain that to the parent. Sometimes, as the saying goes, it is only from the mouths of babes that some parents will actually believe what has happened.

Don't Focus Solely on the Infraction

In our opinion, one of the first rules of doing discipline is that you should take advantage of having a captive audience. Although discipline is the reason you have called a student to your office, you would be remiss as a professional if you focused solely on that. We understand how easy it is to feel overwhelmed by everything on your plate, but it is important that you, as well as your students, see yourself as more than just a disciplinarian. So always keep in mind that one of the main reasons you became an administrator was to improve student achievement, and "disciplining students is truly an instructional activity" (Daresh, 2004, p. 38).

To that end, you might find it beneficial to start or end a conversation with your student with a discussion about how she is doing in her classes. It is equally important that you take an academic interest, rather than just a "behavioral interest," in your students; nor can you take it for granted that her teacher or even her parent(s) pay attention to her grades, so if you can demonstrate a genuine concern in that area, you're showing her that you care about her as a person and about her future and not just as a referral to process. And there is a good chance that if she believes that you will be keeping tabs on her grades, she may very well be motivated to do better.

Before you make a decision about a student and her discipline, you should "solicit information about [her] behavior, work habits, trends in achievement, absences, and tardiness" (Simpson, 2000, p. 94) from her teachers and counselors both to form a fuller picture of what you are seeing as well as to determine if there is a pattern of behavior; such information can also help you yield possible solutions. It is helpful to review your student's record prior to her coming to you so that you can ask her a specific question, such as, "What's going on in geometry?" "Why did your grade drop in English this last marking period?" or "What are you doing to improve in chemistry?" Ideally, there will be occasions when you'll be able to recognize the student for improvement in her grades, attendance, or both.

If you're unable to highlight the student's academic improvement, what is important is that you acknowledge something positive about him when you see him for disciplinary consequences. We know that can be difficult, so if you are unable to comment on his grades, attendance, or an improvement in one of his classes, try to recall something about his extracurricular or personal life that you can bring up. You might be able to reference his role in the school play, his rushing performance in last week's football game, or his new job. Regardless of what you choose to highlight, you need to find something positive or attempt to make some kind of personal connection so that the student won't feel as though every visit to your office beats him down.

Recognize the Student's Effort to Communicate

Once the student has done a thorough job of explaining the situation, you may consider saying something to the effect of, "You know, when I first heard about this incident, I was so upset and disappointed that I was automatically going to give you X as a consequence. After talking with you and confirming your statement, I want you to know that I am now leaning more toward giving you Y, which I think is fair." This helps the student see the value of open communication even when she has done something wrong. If she is punished for being open, she will receive the opposite message.

WORK WITH YOUR STUDENTS

As is the case for classroom teachers, there are some crucial (and sometimes obvious yet overlooked) techniques for working with your students in situations ranging from the ordinary to the tense (and intense). How you choose to work with them in these situations can have a profound impact on the outcome; your rapport with your students, parents, and staff; and the resulting disciplinary consequences.

Don't Assume

It is an unfortunate reality that when you receive a referral, you cannot simply assume that the teacher is right. We wish we could tell you that every referral from a teacher represents an accurate description of what occurred, that the teacher is not at fault, or that the teacher could not have avoided or prevented the situation in the first place, but we'd be lying if we did. Understandably, this sounds cynical, but the truth of the matter is that we all are human, and when it comes to classroom misbehavior and discipline, they are about personalities and perceptions, so the truth can very easily be lost in the process. We therefore encourage you to "investigate" the referral you are addressing. Although this rule of thumb is unlikely to hold true for major infractions, you would be surprised by how often teachers *swear* that a student skipped their class when in fact he was actually present and can provide different kinds of evidence in his defense. By demonstrating to the student that you are willing to look into the situation and defer consequences until you have done so, you are effectively telling him that you are impartial, that you are willing to listen to him, that you don't already have your mind made up when he walks into your office. (Students will also recognize how valuable your time is, so you also earn a measure of respect by essentially agreeing to call him down to your office again or dedicate more time than you had anticipated to the situation.)

Just Listen

Sometimes students simply need you to listen to them. When you're busy or because you are in charge, it is very easy to forget this simple truth: in general, students just want to be heard—so we can use reminding from time to time to talk less and listen more. But in a disciplinary setting, it is even more important to be able to listen to what students have to say. And even when they are wrong, some students might need someone just to listen to them *unload*. Many times in our experience, even when students are in the wrong, by the time they have finished venting and unloading, they ultimately admit they were wrong: they just needed a sounding board against which to work out their frustrations. They may ultimately express appreciation for your listening and often do not even question the consequences, which, if they had been cut off early on, they would have surely fought.

Give Reasons

Take a step outside yourself and consider for a moment how much you hated the following phrase (and perhaps still do): "Because I said so." Well, the same holds true for your students. A related peeve for them is "Because I'm in charge." Instead of employing these tired expressions, treat your students as adults and with respect by explaining your thought process and your rationale. Let them understand that your decisions are not arbitrary and that you would like to treat them almost like colleagues by explaining yourself.

Know When to Give Space

As we are both dog lovers, we often make comparisons to students and dogs—not in a negative way but in a very respectful way: both crave structure and consistency, both need to be able to respect their leader, both can sniff out the true person they have standing in front of them, and, in most cases, both are willing to forgive if they are convinced you care about them. Along those lines, students too will give you warning signs when they are annoyed, upset, and mad. Learn to read those signs, so that when you see them, much like a dog's raised hackles or its tail between its legs, you will know that it's not only appropriate to back away and give them space but in fact essential to do so. If you fail to heed these signs, you run the risk of escalating the situation and being unable to resolve it satisfactorily.

Don't Yell

Although it is generally necessary to be firm, and sometimes you may need to be a bit loud in order to be heard, very rarely do students deserve to be yelled at. Nevertheless, we've known colleagues with short fuses who readily yell at students during a confrontation or in response to the student's yelling. Once you counter with yelling, you run the risk of losing control (and the student's respect) or at least of being perceived as having lost control, and some students will gladly go along for that ride. Rather, we have found it more productive to respond in those situations with a very controlled, staccato tone rather than a raised voice. And if you're still not convinced, consider this: if someone witnessed your yelling, wouldn't she have to wonder who the adult was in the room? So when possible, lower your voice. Allow the student to rant and rave as you would a small child having a tantrum, and instead simply ask, "Are you done?"

Use Body Language

Students might not always hear what you are saying, but they will believe what they are seeing. Thus an important way of handling your students in a disciplinary setting is by utilizing body language and nonverbal cues. For example, the teacher favorite, the "hairy eyeball," or a stern, disapproving look, works just as well in the office as it does in the classroom and can convey disappointment, disapproval, and displeasure much more eloquently than yelling can. We're sure you recall using proximity in the classroom to corral students who were off task, and this idea can be used just as effectively in an office setting, but with a twist. For example, you might choose one moment to sit behind your desk in order to erect a barrier that establishes your authority, but the next moment to sit across from them to express compassion and help pick up the pieces.

Don't Bluff 'em

A surefire way to quickly lose credibility with your students is by bluffing them. For example, if you have no intention of suspending the student for similar future infractions, then you should never threaten him with that as a disciplinary consequence. It's easy to think that you're talking tough, but don't fool yourself: more than likely, someone will eventually call your bluff. When he does, you are then headed down a slippery slope, being unfair by handing down an incommensurate consequence in order to stand by your word and save face. And you will quickly learn that if you don't follow through with what you had originally stated, your credibility will be greatly diminished. Students won't know when (if ever) to really believe what you're saying about consequences, and staff won't be sure that they can trust you to discipline students (or may see you as weak for not backing up your threats).

Never Send Students Immediately Back to Class

No matter how effective and efficient you might be in handling your discipline, you should never send a student immediately back to class if she had been sent to see you by her classroom teacher. Although you might view quick turnaround time as evidence of your efficiency, you run the risk of alienating the teacher because he might view your swiftness as a lack of dealing with the student or not taking the situation seriously enough. So even if you are finished with a student who was sent to the office, wait at least fifteen minutes before having her go back to class (Curwin, Mendler, and Mendler, 2008). We realize that you don't want your students missing valuable instructional time, but giving the student (and teacher) time apart to cool down is just as important: learning cannot occur when a student is so annoyed or upset that she can't see straight.

Curwin, Mendler, and Mendler (2008) also point out that "teachers really appreciate the administrator accompanying a student back to the classroom, which tends to minimize an inappropriate reentry" (p. 81). You send a message to the rest of the class when you accompany the student back. Moreover, many students who return to the classroom unescorted tend to boast, "Nothing happened to me," which, even if it is untrue, creates a perception in the classroom that neither you nor the teacher want, so walking back with him helps minimize this. In addition, it is important that you "help the student come up with a plan for how he is going to behave upon returning" (p. 101) to his class. Even if you give the student a "time-out" and escort him back to class, there is always the possibility that his emotions can get the best of him upon returning, especially if he feels he has been "wronged."

Educators and laymen alike would probably argue that the main responsibility of a school administrator is to improve student achievement. With such terms as *instructional leader* and *learning leader* prominent in educational literature, it is ostensibly difficult to disagree with experts and other stakeholders. However, we tend to subscribe to a more paradoxical notion of the primary responsibility of administrators. Indeed, student achievement is paramount, and it is critical for administrators to work with their collaborative teams, conduct classroom observations, and provide support to help coach novice and veteran teachers alike (or to create documentation for the dismissal of teachers who are not a good match for the profession). But at the same time, good instruction cannot occur if there is not a physically and emotionally safe learning environment. And therein lies what we believe is your primary responsibility: ensuring a safe learning environment—a place where students do not ruin the learning opportunities for others; a place where students feel comfortable offering answers without fear of intimidation, bullying, or mockery; a place where professionals do not need to be subjected to intimidation, bullying, or mockery and are able to facilitate learning uninterrupted; a place where there is a positive learning environment for all stakeholders so that they need not worry about emotional or physical harm.

In your efforts to establish such an environment, you are bound to encounter and create conflict with both students and staff. Early on, this is an unsettling feeling, as you are working in their best interest, which many will not understand and some will even refuse to believe. The best advice we can give you for these instances, or for the more contentious meetings in your office, is to learn not to take things personally—to develop a thick skin. This is easier said than done, but we suggest that you follow the advice of Curwin, Mendler, and Mendler (2008), who recommend reacting as if the student (or teacher even!) had just "called you a chair" (p. 133). This is an essential leadership skill that you need to learn: stoicism. You must be able to present a calm demeanor, remain unflappable, and not allow what people say and how they act to push your buttons or get under your skin. And even when they succeed, you need to be able to convey a sense of calm and coolheadedness. Once you can, handling your discipline will become easier and a little less stressful for you, and it will put you on the path toward "constructing a school or classroom that encourages curriculum, activities, and interactions to address the basic needs of connection, competence, and control" (p. 44).

Conducting Investigations

*I*t's been a steadily busy morning, but overall a relatively quiet one. You were able to knock out a few e-mails, return some phone calls, meet with a couple of teachers who had concerns about the new tardy policy, set up a meeting with a local business about developing a partnership, and even address a few routine referrals. But all that changes without a second's notice. Before you can make it into the hall at the class change to go to your cafeteria duty, you are frantically summoned to the main hallway: there has been a fight.

The hallway hums with electricity, and upon your arrival, a circle of students quickly begins to disperse, revealing two teachers who have managed to separate and restrain two boys who had been fighting. One of the students has some blood on his face and visible welts. Is he the victim or the aggressor? *you wonder as you make way to the scene.* Tensions are high, and even though he has been restrained, one student continues to provoke the other by taunting, challenging, and insulting him. Onlookers linger and are reluctant to go to class, thinking—almost hoping—that there might be a second round, which they certainly don't want to miss.

Friends chatter excitedly about what they witnessed—and what they think they witnessed—while news of the fight is exaggerated and makes its way to the classes in the next period. Two teachers assist in bringing the students to the main office to ensure that simmering tempers do not reignite another fight, and now in the main office with the two students, you find yourself having to conduct an investigation into what exactly happened, which will most likely take up the entire period if not longer. So much for the cafeteria duty and the quick observation you had planned.

Because the word *investigation* has such a negative connotation to it, many educators prefer using the term *fact finding*. Whatever it is called, it refers to the process of identifying objective details about an incident and determining what happened to whom and, most important, why. The more concrete the details you gather, the more likely you are to find a way to reach a resolution. In most cases, you will reserve this level of inquiry for the more serious infractions, such as threats, fights, substance offenses, serious disagreements, or other issues that are more complicated than, say, a student's simply skipping a class. We are not suggesting that this level of investigative work is inappropriate for the lighter discipline issues; rather, we have just found that in many of the lighter cases, it is unnecessary.

MANAGE YOUR INVESTIGATION

The success of your investigation often hinges on how and when you begin it. The longer you wait or the later it is before someone brings an issue to you, the colder your leads grow, the hazier people's memories become, and the murkier the story becomes as rumors spread. In the example that opened the chapter, however, before starting in on the details of your investigation, you must make a quick assessment of any student who appears to have visible injuries—should he see the school nurse immediately? (Also be sure to have the nurse document the student's injuries for you.) Does he need more serious medical attention? With so much going on at once, we encourage you to ignore as much as possible such distracters as e-mail or voicemail and devote your attention and resources to starting your investigation off on the right foot.

Get Coverage

It always seems that major incidents occur when you are already juggling three other things, have someone on hold on the phone, and need to be somewhere else for a meeting. Large problems rarely appear on a slow day in the main office, nor do they wait for when your schedule has an opening. In our scenario, it goes without saying that you will need to find someone else to cover your cafeteria duty for you, but what is easy to overlook is finding coverage for the adults who witnessed the situation.

Before you even talk with the students who were involved, first find out which adults were in the vicinity of the incident so that you can obtain the most bias-free accounts and statements. If you have a substitute available in the main office, send her to the teacher's class to cover for him so that the two of you can talk. If not, find someone in his department who is off that period who can cover the class for him. Although we don't like infringing on instructional time or instructional planning time, it is better to secure a statement from the teacher as quickly as possible, both to lessen the possibility that the facts will become distorted and to allow you to continue your investigation. A statement from one of your staff members will hold extraordinary weight with parents, district personnel, and even the police if necessary, so it is essential that you get these staff members to immediately record what they observed.

Take Statements

Just as you are finding staff members to talk with, you must simultaneously find student witnesses from whom you can get statements. Aside from asking staff members whom they recall seeing nearby, you should ask each participant in the incident whom they can name as being in the area or passing through. Doing so eliminates accusations that you spoke only with friends of one of the students involved and the like.

Once you have brought student witnesses to the main office, it's best to keep them from interacting with one another to preserve the purity of their individual statements, so be sure to separate them immediately. You don't want their recollection to be tainted by their friend's recollection, nor do you want to allow them the chance to collaborate on their statements. It's also important to keep them apart so that you can compare the veracity of each of the statements and separately ask each student clarifying questions about what he or she wrote. Be sure to ask them to be descriptive, to tell you a vivid story, including as many details as possible; even if obscene language was used, request that they include verbatim the actual words used. We've found that some students are more apt to write a lengthier, more detailed statement if they have access to a computer. We've also found it helpful to have students draw a diagram indicating where the action occurred, who was standing where, and so on; students might get their stories straight with each other in advance of being asked to write statements, but most aren't prepared for making sure their diagrams are the same, so having them draw can be helpful in determining the truth.

When you do call down student witnesses, be sure that you have the main participants in holding somewhere else—it is critical that they be unable to see who is providing you with information. The same holds true for witnesses who are named by each of the participants. Some students are uneasy when asked to write statements, so you might need to assure them that you will not be sharing their written statement or their identity with the students involved. In fact, we've found that citing student privacy—that you are compelled to maintain their anonymity—can be helpful in assuaging their fears. And for those students who are nervous, it is a good public relations move to call their parents to inform them that you needed to enlist their help in resolving a situation that occurred at school.

Naturally, getting the statements of those students who were actively involved in the incident is crucial. You will discover that they too might be reluctant to put in writing what happened. Some students often express concern over being seen as a "snitch" or seen as running to you for your help. It is important that you explain what a snitch *actually* is, in contrast to a person who does her duty to the school and to herself. You can make the situation a teachable moment by drawing a parallel to the civic duty she has to her town and to her country. You might also explain how writing a statement is her right—that you are making sure that she receives due process—and explain what that notion means. You should of course remind her that because you're going to have the other partici-pant's version, it would be helpful if you had her version as well so that you're not getting a one-sided perspective.

Most students will eventually write a statement, but you will always encounter a few who still refuse to do so. Calling their parents and explaining the situation and their refusal to write often helps. For any remaining difficult students, we recommend that rather than outwardly fight them about it, instead explain that not to make a statement is also their right, but that it might ultimately help them if you can explain to the supervisor (or even the police) that they were coopera-tive, that they were forthcoming and were able to assist you. And when that fails, writing on the top of their blank paper "Refused to write" will sometimes cause students to want to write a statement. If they still refuse, you might want to have a second adult sign as a witness to this refusal.

Although they are few in number, we've also known some parents who actively encourage their student not to write a statement. In extreme cases, these parents have stated that no one should be able to talk with their child until they or their legal counsel is present. Although you might want to check with your district's leadership regarding this issue, we operate under the assumption that we are an educational organization, not a law enforcement entity: if we need to talk to a student to ascertain the truth, to ensure the smooth operation of the school, then we will.

Interview Students

Even if you have good statements, you still need to be able to effectively question the key players involved. As a good rule of thumb, you should give as little information as possible and instead let them provide as much information as possible. For the most part, students will talk and will assume that you know what they know, especially if it is about something as public as a fight. Or you might offer only a little bit of information to create the illusion that you know what they know. Much of your approach will depend on the situation, but you will soon discover that you can stitch together what actually happened while only possessing swatches of information.

With so much information coming in to you, be sure to take notes and even make notes on the students' statements; it is essential that you have your information and facts straight before you proceed. When you do start, one of the simplest yet best openings you can use is, "Do you know why I called you to my office?" You will find that most students will sheepishly admit they know why, and many will enthusiastically begin giving you important details about what happened. Even more effective can be purposely using the first word in this next statement: "*Help* me understand what went on." And of course you want to determine *why* the incident occurred as well as what actually transpired, and with any luck, the students will fill in the blanks along the way.

You are also looking for discrepancies among students' stories. Keep the following in mind when questioning students or reviewing statements:

- Does the student deviate from what he originally said or wrote?
- Are there any discrepancies among the details in his version of what happened?
- Are there discrepancies between one participant's story and another's?
- Are there discrepancies between one witness's statement and another's?
- Are there discrepancies among the witnesses' statements and those of the participants?

Aside from discrepancies, you also are trying to answer the following:

- What can one student confirm about another's statement?
- What details or information has been corroborated by everyone involved?

Search Students

In keeping with the scenario at the start of the chapter, you might find yourself in a situation where you need to search a student. The issue of searching students is a delicate one. Even in the past decade, administrators still have regularly run afoul of the law and students' rights in this area, as evidenced by several high-profile cases in which students were strip-searched by school administrators. So when we discuss searching a student, we absolutely do not mean a strip search: under no circumstance do we recommend that a school official pursue this action. "Except for emergency situations posing immediate danger to the safety of students, few circumstances appear to necessitate such intrusions" (McCarthy, Cambron-McCabe, and Thomas, 1998, p. 226), but even when such situations arise, we suggest that you contact a supervisor for some direction. We also aren't talking about a "pat-down," which might be permissible in many school systems and states; again, you don't want to put yourself in a vulnerable position where a student could fabricate a damaging accusation against you. Rather, we are talking about your right and need to see what the student has on his person or in his possession.

Know When (and When Not) to Search   One of the most obvious but also most important guidelines is never to conduct a search alone; you always want to have a second person, preferably another administrator, present as a witness. And one of you should be the same gender as the student. Your decision to search a student must be based on your having a "reasonable suspicion" of the need to do so—"specific and articulable facts, which taken together with rational inferences from the facts, justify a warrantless search" (McCarthy, Cambron-McCabe, and Thomas, 1998, p. 499). The reasonableness of a search is determined by the reliability of the information that led to the search, "exigency to make the search without delay and further investigation" (p. 219), the seriousness of the problem, and the student's record, among other factors; ultimately, you must have more than "a hunch, good intentions, or good faith" (p. 219).

For example, if a teacher reported that someone stole a cell phone from a girl's purse and no one witnessed it, you would not have grounds, or reasonable suspicion, to search anyone (and especially not everyone) in the classroom. Searching the entire class is tantamount to a baseless search and will immediately land you in hot water. However, if the teacher reported that she observed a student loitering near the other student's desk or in the vicinity just prior to the student's realizing her phone was missing, and he had no business being in that part of the classroom, then you might have reasonable suspicion for a search. But keep in mind that rather than immediately launching into a search, you would want to begin by simply interviewing the student.

Ask, "Do You Have Anything on You That You Shouldn't Have?" Leading into your search by asking students this question is helpful in a couple of regards. First, before you even explain the concept of "reasonable suspicion" to the student (which we urge you to do before you begin a search), asking this simple question causes many students to *offer* to empty their pockets or volunteer to a search; we've found that students will quickly reply, "Not at all—you can even search me," and sometimes before you can even respond, they start emptying their pockets onto the table. Keep in mind that their willingness in this situation does not always mean that they are not carrying something on them that they shouldn't; some students will attempt to use this as a bluff against a search or are overconfident about how well they have hidden the contraband. Ultimately, though, it is always better when they are helpful and cooperative, or volunteer to a search. Another important thing to keep in mind is that in many districts, you need the student's permission or consent to be subject to a search.

The second, even more important reason to open with this question is that it is a blanket statement. In essence, you might be searching for a knife from the fight, but what if you find a bag of marijuana over the course of your search? Although the student would most definitely receive consequences from the school, what he might actually be more in need of is to be involved in the court system with supervised probation. So we've always operated on the assumption that a good lawyer is on the lookout for a loophole: if you don't use this kind of broad questioning, some attorneys may say that the contraband is not admissible in court because the marijuana wasn't what you were originally looking for. We are not offering legal advice—only sharing a situation that we have experienced in the past.

If after you've asked the opening question the student does not consent to a search, then you have a difficult decision to make. In some districts, it is permissible to suspend the student on the grounds of insubordination or defiance. In some situations, the student's refusal might necessitate a phone call to local law enforcement for their assistance. You should be sure to receive clarification from your district on how to proceed in this instance.

Know What to Search   You may (or may not) be surprised by the ingenuity of some students, so it is imperative that you know what to search. First, the courts have upheld that you are able to search a student's locker if you have reasonable suspicion (as opposed to conducting random searches of all lockers) because "there is a lower expectation of privacy, frequently distinguishing locker searches on the basis that a locker is school property, and a student does not retain exclusive possession" (McCarthy, Cambron-McCabe, and Thomas, 1998, p. 221). If you are going to search a locker, you should again have a witness present as well as the student (and we've often asked the student to open the locker for us and then step back so that we can inspect it).

When it comes to deciding whether to search a student's belongings, keep in mind that students have "a higher expectation of privacy in their personal property or effects than in their school lockers" (McCarthy, Cambron-McCabe, and Thomas, 1998, p. 223). These instances require more specificity or an "individualized suspicion that a violation of a law or school rule has occurred" (p. 223). Finally, a "student's car, like other personal possessions, may be searched if reasonable suspicion can be established" (p. 224).

In terms of actually conducting a search, it entails looking at things in ways you might never have thought of before. The following is a list of the kinds of containers and other objects you might want to consider examining over the course of a search, depending on the situation or infraction:

- *Pockets.* As an obvious starting point, have students empty the contents of their pockets and then make bunny ears with the insides of their pockets. It is nearly impossible to do this to a back pocket, and students know this: have them pull the pocket open so that you can see inside it. If your district permits you to put your hands inside a student's pockets, first ask the student if there is anything in it that might be sharp or dangerous; when you put your hand inside the pocket, it is a good idea to do so with your palm facing *away* from the student's body. (Remember to have your witness observe.)

- *Wallet.* Most people would not consider that a wallet would contain contraband, but small sheets of acid, a pouch of cocaine, or even a razor blade could be carefully hidden in between a driver's license and school ID card.

- *Shoes.* Students (and novice administrators) are surprised when we ask students to remove their shoes, but haven't you at some point tucked money inside your shoes when traveling? Be sure to see the bottom of the student's feet, as items might be stored inside the socks, and also inspect under the shoe inserts, lining, and tongue.

- *Pant cuffs.* For some students, it is fashionable to cuff their pants with rubber bands or shoelaces, so be sure to ask them to remove these in case they are serving to keep something from sliding out of the pants. If the pants have cuffs, have the student turn them inside out as well.

- *Shirtsleeves.* A long-sleeve knit shirt is ideal for hiding a small bag of drugs. Have students pull the sleeve away from the wrist and then shake their sleeve. If the sleeves are rolled up, have the student unroll them.

- *Hat.* If your school does not have a no-hat policy, ask the student to remove his or her hat, and be sure to check inside the sweatband at the base of the hat as well as the lining.

- *Waistband.* Long, baggy shirts can be used to conceal something in the waist, so ask the student to run his hands through his waistband just to be safe. Also, weapons or holsters could be clipped to belts.

- *Belt and belt buckle.* Again, this is one of those areas that you probably never thought of, but there are belt buckles designed to contain a blade right in the buckle itself and accessible with just a flick of the wrist. Of course the ordinary money belt is also a great hiding place; they are old-fashioned, but still exist.

- *Backpack.* Many students are too savvy to leave contraband in their locker because they know that by law, unannounced drug sweeps with canines can be conducted, so they keep their belongings on them, rarely housing anything in their lockers. Be sure to check all compartments in the backpack, as many of them have small, concealed pockets. We've even known students to slice the lining and sew their own pockets inside!

- *Pens, mechanical pencils, and markers.* Most of these writing implements are hollow inside, so drugs are easy to stash inside them; you might want to take them apart, especially because they are so easy to take apart and reassemble.

- *Lipstick, lip balm, and the like.* Again, these items are hollow inside. Moreover, many male students have their female friends hold contraband for them because they are less likely to be suspected, accused, and searched. In addition, there are some containers designed to look like lipstick that are actually knives in disguise, so you might even want to remove the cap just to be on the safe side.

- *Books.* Students often don't believe that you'll think to look in a book. Books, including their covers and bindings, and even a notebook or loose-leaf binder all have the capacity for concealing items.

- *Cigarette pack and lighter.* It might sound obvious, but we know people who have made this mistake: don't assume that cigarette packs contain just cigarettes. It's always a good idea not only to look inside the pack of cigarettes but also to shake out the tobacco in the cigarettes (or cigar) to see if there is a change in color from brown to green, which can indicate the presence of marijuana. In addition, when emptied of their lighter fluid, some lighters can be taken apart to hold pills or small quantities of other illegal substances. You might even want to cautiously try using the lighter: they can sometimes be disguised electric shocking devices and even as switchblades.

- *Cell phone and PDA.* We include this not to recommend that you search the actual cell phone but to encourage you to *look closely* at the cell phone. A few years ago, law enforcement made school officials aware of several different types of homemade guns, some of which resemble cell phones— some even to the point that they were "foldable" and could be clipped to the inside front pocket such that they would look like cell phone clips to observers.

- *Locker.* Be sure to feel behind the frame of the door and underneath the top shelf; check to see if the floor of the locker can be easily pried up. Use caution here, though: not only do some lockers have very sharp edges, but students can also conceal open-edge razorblades in these hidden areas.

- *Car.* It is fairly obvious to look inside the door and seat pockets, but be sure to check inside change dishes and in and under ashtrays, examine cigarette lighters, look under floor mats, and inspect other less conspicuous areas.

When you look through a student's backpack or locker, obviously you want to open up anything that could have a compartment or the ability to hide something. This even includes common objects like camcorders, cameras, or even cases for cell phones and iPods. You might even encounter such random items as screwdrivers, tire pressure gauges, and even dipsticks! If you ask someone from law enforcement, he or she will surely confirm that all of these have been reported as either concealed objects or as doubling as weapons. That is why we encourage you to talk with your school resource officer (SRO) if you have one, because as the more knowledgeable school administrators become, the more savvy the rule breakers become. And if an object seems out of place in a student's possession, it is always best to err on the side of caution. Examine the item and, when in doubt, hold on to it and ask the parent to come in to pick it up.

Make Parental Contact

An important rule of thumb is never to leave the building with unfinished business. What this means when you investigate a major infraction or give serious consequences is that it is essential to call the parents before the day ends. You don't want the student arriving home and being the first to inform the parents about what happened. Can you imagine how a parent would react if she heard from her child that he was searched on suspicion of drug possession and she never heard from you about it? If the situation you dealt with has potential legal or criminal ramifications, you should also inform the parents that you are compelled to report the incident to the police. Make it clear to them that you don't have any control over that aspect of the matter; many parents will be inquisitive about what the police will do or how they handle it, and the best response is usually something along the lines of, "I can't predict what they will do, but I will be sure to express to them how helpful and cooperative your child was over the course of my investigation."

Document Evidence

Once you turn over the evidence to law enforcement (if this is necessary), it is not your evidence anymore. Make sure that before you do so, you take and print the necessary pictures of the evidence. We cannot stress enough the need for being able to produce photographic evidence of the student's infraction. This would be especially important if a family member were to appeal your decision all the way to the school board. For example, be sure not only to photograph a knife you confiscate but also to place it up against a ruler so that it is clear how large it is. Or if you find marijuana on a student and it happens to be in small baggies inside a larger bag, you would want to take out the small bags and photograph them instead of just photographing the larger bag. The important thing to take away from this is to be sure to immediately document whatever evidence you have; more important, if it is an illegal item, immediately transfer the property to the SRO after you have documented it.

Report to the Police

Anytime there is an infraction that occurs in school (and sometimes even outside of school) that is illegal—involving drugs, alcohol, assaults, weapons, illicit behavior, and threats, to mention a few—you are required to report it to the police (although we do urge you to check your specific district and state policies about this). In fact, we make it a point to be transparent about this topic: while we are explaining the school-based consequences, we tell students and their parents that we are also obligated to inform the police about the offense as well. For example, if you hear that a student has been drinking alcohol in school and are able to verify it, you need to report this to your SRO after you impose disciplinary consequences. Doing so is nonnegotiable, and we encourage you to check with your district as to how long you have to report an offense as well as what to do if you don't have an SRO in your building.

The proper handling of evidence is a critical aspect of notifying law enforcement of reportable infractions. First of all, never leave contraband in your office overnight, and never transport this kind of evidence yourself. We've known misguided staff members who, trying to do the right thing, drove illegal substances to the police station themselves after school hours. Some have even kept evidence in their desks until they were able to speak with law enforcement. Our general philosophy is that once you are done with an investigation, you need to "punt" the evidence as soon as possible. You should not hold on to any kind contraband any longer than you have to, let alone carry it around on your person or in your car—we mention this only because we've known more than one administrator who has done that. And if you have no one in your building who can relieve you of it, then we recommend calling the police and requesting that someone come to the school to claim the items; otherwise, you are now the one in illegal possession.

ADDRESS POSTDISCIPLINE CONCERNS

By this point in an investigation, you will have made a determination with regard to administering severe consequences. Warnings, lunch detention, detention halls, removal of privileges, and even in-school restriction generally are not commensurate with an infraction that triggered a full-blown investigation. Rather, we are talking about a consequence that removes the student from the instructional environment: an out-of-school suspension, long-term suspension, or a recommendation of expulsion. Once the student is sent home, it is most tempting to just move on—the student has been suspended, and now you are able to get back to your other business. But that student will eventually be coming back to you; how will you address that?

Hold a Reinstatement

Some school districts require the suspended student and his parents to meet with an administrator before he returns to school, or is "reinstated," at the end of his suspension. However, there is often little guidance as to what to do in these meetings other than to adhere to the requirement that they be held. Even if your district does not require a reinstatement meeting, we still believe you should hold one, because it is an opportunity to meet under more favorable circumstances and to set some ground rules, reinforce expectations, and provide some support, counseling, and advice, depending on the infraction.

When you are finishing up your suspension paperwork and speaking with the parents, inform them that there will be a reinstatement meeting on such-and-such a date that they must attend in order for their child to come back to school. (Be sure that your suspension letter restates this and names the date and time of the meeting.) Because the parents will most likely have to take off work, you need to be sure that they feel that the meeting time is well spent and of importance. This is a chance for parents to leave the school thinking, "Wow—they really are trying to help my child." It is also an opportunity to include the parents as partners and to solicit their help in problem solving.

Have the Student Explain Why He or She Was Suspended We like to begin reinstatement meetings by stating their purpose to the student and parents: "The purpose of this reinstatement is to review the events that led up to the suspension as well as to discuss strategies to avoid a reoccurrence." We then ask the student to explain in her own words why she was suspended. It is important to have her do this because we want her to see that the suspension was a result of her own behavior and not the fault of someone else, and to recognize that what she did was wrong.

Help the Student Identify Plans A crucial part of the reinstatement is to help the student identify what alternatives he has to engaging in the behavior that landed him in that predicament to begin with. Help him identify alternative plans by asking the questions that we posed in Chapter Three, such as what he could do differently if he could do it all over again or if he found himself in a similar situation. Encourage him to name staff members whom he would feel comfortable approaching and confiding in if he found himself in a precarious situation, so that he understands that he has resources and assistance available to him to help him avoid making the same mistakes.

Ask, "What Can I Do to Help?"   We know that you want to see your students succeed. One of the best ways to demonstrate your caring is simply to ask them how you can help. In the context of a reinstatement meeting, asking the student, "What can I do to help?" can show that although you had to conduct some ugly business, you truly do care about her well-being and want to be able to help her. This question also prompts the student to identify what she needs in order to be successful; this is far more effective than your imposing sanctions of which she has no ownership and buy-in.

Clarify and Reinforce Expectations   The reinstatement is an ideal time to revisit the school's rules and regulations and to stress what won't be tolerated by you, the school system, and (you hope) the parents. Specify the behavior that you are seeking as well as the behavior that you are discouraging. You should also explain future consequences to the student and parents for future infractions.

Solicit Parents' Support   The reinstatement meeting is a prime opportunity to invite parents into a partnership, so be sure to include them in the meeting. One simple way is to ask them what questions they have—either about the infraction and consequence or about its impact. But you can also solicit their support by making them aware of other resources they might have available to them if they continue to see undesirable behavior at home. Also inform them that if they become aware of information indicating that the infraction has not been laid to rest, then they should contact you immediately so that you can be aware of it and guide them in the proper direction if the situation is outside your purview. Finally, you can also ask them if they feel there is anything you can do to help their child acclimate to being back in school and stay on the straight and narrow.

Verify Contact Information   Because people change phone numbers so often (especially if their cell phone is their primary number), the reinstatement meeting is a good time to verify and update the contact information you have on file for the parents.

Organize for Appeals

Your objective is not to have any of your disciplinary decisions appealed. But with that said, there are always going to be instances where parents do not agree with the discipline their child received. Whether they think that their child has been disciplined without due process, that the consequence assigned is too severe, or that their child is innocent, you will need to pull together information for the appeal. Your district may have formal guidelines for how to prepare information, but if it doesn't, the following sections will be of help.

Grades   When hearing an appeal, the arbiter can benefit from having a picture of the student's overall standing in school; grades are one piece of that picture. However, grades should not be an excuse to decrease or increase a consequence; they should serve only to gain a better understanding of the student's overall success at school. In addition, your referencing a student's grades during an appeal allows you to demonstrate not just an interest in a single infraction but a sincere concern for the student as a whole person. Although you can access grades through the school's student information system, you will obtain a more current and accurate snapshot by distributing a request to the student's teachers for the most up-to-date information about his progress and behavior.

Attendance   Presenting a student's attendance data is another way to get to know her outside the discipline infraction. A student's attendance record should include absences—excused and unexcused—and tardies as well.

Discipline Record   This record should identify whether the infraction is the student's first or a reflection of a pattern of behavior and offenses. An accurate discipline record can be extremely helpful if it shows a logical sequence in the severity of infractions and consequences. For example, the record could indicate that a fair and reasonable approach has been followed to help this student conform to school policy; this can be documented by including all attempts at curbing the student's misbehavior—phone calls home, parent conferences, teacher conferences, and referrals to internal and external resources (guidance counselors, mental health agencies, the courts, and so on).

Details   A report of the details of the infraction should show a sequence of events, timelines, dates, and an overall breach of conduct and its consequences. Because the arbiter is not likely to want (or to have the time) to be fully briefed on the situation, a simple table can provide him or her with the essential information and sequence of events that led up to the consequence. You would want to include in the table the basic information: what happened, where it took place, and when it took place. It is also helpful (but not mandatory) to include when you first started working on the case, at what point the parents were contacted, and evidence that the student had an opportunity to explain his version of the incident before you made a decision about the consequence.

Precedent   If the case being appealed is particularly difficult, complex, or unusual, it might be helpful if you were to provide the reviewer with information about similar situations that have occurred with other students or administrators at your school. Doing so can indicate that you are trying to stay in line with consequences for similar offenses.

Reconnect

Because of the seriousness of the infraction and the consequence, it would be foolish to assume that your relationship with your student will simply revert to what it was without some additional nurturing and support.

Check In with the Student   Set aside time to check in with your student who had received consequences. Depending on the infraction and his reaction, you might choose to do so the day after he arrives back to school, by the end of the week, or a couple of weeks later. There is no hard-and-fast rule here: you know your students, so you should know what would be acceptable.

Checking in is not difficult. You could send a pass for him, see him informally before or after school, or touch base with him in the cafeteria. What is important is that he sees that you took time from your schedule to fit him into it.

Follow Up with the Parents   Just as it is important to check in with your student after she returns from a suspension, it is equally important to follow up with her parents. Set aside a few minutes to call the parents to inquire how their student is behaving at home or whether they are aware of any new concerns. It is also good public relations simply to call home and tell the parents that you had touched base with their child to see how she was doing upon returning from her suspension. The advantage to this kind of phone call is that it is positive, in pleasant contrast to the call you had to make to inform them about the suspension.

We are confident that you're familiar with the notion that teachers aren't just teachers, that they wear many hats. They are also counselors, nurses, social workers, advocates, role models, mentors, and parents, just to name a few roles. The same holds true for an administrator. At times you must be a policeman, detective, attorney, judge, and probation officer. Even though you might not relish wearing those hats, these roles are a necessary component of your ensuring a safe learning environment for both students and staff. And if you are able to demonstrate an ability to conduct smooth and fair investigations (while still tending to your other responsibilities), you will earn significant credibility with your teachers and parents.

PART TWO

Working with Adults

Creating and Maintaining Parent Partnerships

*Y*ou have just returned to school after having been out all morning at a district-level training; you hope to catch up on your e-mail before the lunch shifts start, just as soon as you visit Mrs. Anderson during her planning period to follow up with her on how her husband is recovering from his surgery. When you reach the work-room, you are called over the radio: a parent is unexpectedly waiting to speak with you in the main office. Her family is new to the area, and she would like to meet with an administrator before registering her son. You make a mental note to see Mrs. Anderson by the end of the day, and return to the main office. But you are surprised to see another set of parents waiting to meet with you when you return to the office. Before you can even introduce yourself to anyone, your secretary tells you that you have a parent on hold; she is uncertain about the nature of the phone call, but the tone of her voice suggests that it is important.

Schools owe much of their success to the involvement of parents. Whether it is in the form of volunteering at the school, serving on boosters, being concerned parents, or simply asking their student how their day was and if she completed her homework, parental support and engagement play an essential role in the school's overall operation and success.

Working with parents as partners in their children's education and formative years can be a rewarding experience, and although there are no real data to confirm this, the majority of parents will be on the same page with you when you work with their children. And as an administrator, you have a high stake in interacting with parents because you do so on such a regular basis, meanwhile attempting the difficult balancing act of keeping both them and your teachers satisfied while also tending to your other professional responsibilities. But just as we tell parents, we administrators are like family too, considering the amount of time that we spend with their children. And like real families, there are bound to be disagreements, especially because although both you and the student's parents have a common bond—the vested interest in seeing the student succeed—you may have differing thoughts on how to achieve that success.

BUILD A FOUNDATION

As you face the daily rigors of your job, you can lose sight of an essential aspect of being an effective administrator: working with parents. Some administrators see this as another example of dealing with the tough stuff because parents are authority figures, and if the administrator is younger than the parent, that adds an additional dynamic for him or her. But parents can also have the same concerns, especially because administrators, too, are authority figures. Therefore, creating a strong foundation with parents is a crucial first step in overcoming these feelings and building a partnership with them.

Eliminate Titles

We ask students to call us Mr., Mrs., or Dr. because it is a sign of respect. These titles also establish us as authority figures in the school, primarily among the students. With that said, why insist on this formality when meeting with or speaking to parents? By eliminating the title and simply introducing yourself with your first and last name as you would if you had just met the friend of a friend, you remove a potential barrier between you and the parent. With this type of introduction, parents can use what they feel is most comfortable to them. Some will prefer to use your surname; others, your first name. In any case, you are now speaking to the parent as *a person* and not as an administrator, which can set a more positive tone and help facilitate dialogue. However, we do urge you to refer to parents by title until they give you permission to use their first name.

Establish a Positive Tone

The atmosphere in the main office has a powerful impact—positive or negative—on your relationship with parents. Meet with the secretaries in order to establish expectations for how visitors are greeted when they enter the main office as well as for phone-answering etiquette. We have found it helpful to ask our front-office staff to picture the most positive experience they've had when entering an office and to list the specifics that made it so. Then together we draw from that list the positive behaviors that should be part of our routine and expected day-to-day etiquette.

Acknowledge Their Time as Being Important

Any time you call a parent, you should consider prefacing your conversation with a very simple statement: "I'm sorry to interrupt your day, but I wouldn't if this weren't important." Whether you call them at work or at home, use the same phrase. Your intention is to acknowledge that your phone call is an unexpected intrusion on their time: no matter how supportive or involved they are, your parents lead busy lives, so it is respectful to make that acknowledgment.

Stage Your Office

Your office possesses inherent barriers that you should seek to eliminate when meeting with parents. For example, your desk is a symbol of power and authority and can be a barrier between you and the parents. If you are seated behind your desk across from parents, you are possibly reminding them of adversarial relationships they had as students, and we're confident that your intention is not to make an adult feel like a student. In fact, we have on several occasions had parents remark upon entering the office that they feel as they did when they were in school and had been called to the office even if they had not been in trouble. Moreover, think of other environments where people sit across from one another: policemen interrogating suspects, lawyers conferring with defendants, judges in a court of law, doctors delivering bad news to patients, separated couples at arbitration, and so on. Parents may find these images or feelings sneaking into their minds when they're seated across a desk from you in your office. If you want your students' parents to be partners with you, then you want to eliminate this avoidable barrier.

Instead, when possible, arrange the chairs so that you are able to sit next to the parents so that there is no object between you. Natural conversation flows better with this kind of configuration, and people let their guard down when you are seated next to them rather than across from them; you will appear more accessible. Sitting next to them also sends an unspoken message that you are willing to collaborate with them and, more important, that you are partners who are working side by side to help their child succeed.

Pretend They Are Your Only Appointment

One of the best doctors we know was recommended to us because "he makes you feel as though you are the only appointment of the day, that there is no one else in the waiting room." In short, he conducts himself in a fashion contrary to most people's experience with doctors. For example, he makes patients feel special and important by actually sitting down and genuinely talking with them and answering questions; he does not rush through his appointment or make his patients feel that they are infringing on his time or inconveniencing him. He books appointments with enough time between them to allow for a consultation that runs long, and he is careful to keep an organized calendar and not double book or overbook clients. For all these reasons, he has consistently been recognized as a top general practitioner in the Washington DC area. His actions sound like simple things, and they are. But as simple as they are, they are not as widespread as one would hope. They don't occur by accident, and they don't occur on a regular basis in either doctors' or administrators' offices.

In *Blink,* Malcolm Gladwell (2005) references a study by Wendy Levinson about the difference between doctors who are and are not sued for malpractice. In essence, the study revealed that doctors who spend more than three minutes longer than the average appointment length of fifteen minutes significantly reduced the risk of being sued for malpractice. (The researchers actually state that these surgeons who spent more time had never been sued.) Their findings? That people tend not to sue someone they like. The study further revealed that the quality of the doctors' care was not the determining factor. Gladwell notes, "The difference was entirely in *how* they talked to their patients" (p. 42), meaning that they demonstrated active listening skills and seemed genuinely interested in what the patient was saying. They were not dismissive, and they made the patients feel as though they were the only ones who mattered. Parents need that level of attention, too. They know you have other students and responsibilities to tend to, but that is not their concern.

Share Positives

To establish a strong foundation, make sure that your parents hear positive news and information about their children from you. One way to do this is to establish a habit of making one positive phone call to a family each week. Although it may sound as though we're setting the bar fairly low, we're trying to be realistic, given the demanding nature of your job. And if you do make just one call, you may find it a little easier to make a second positive phone call immediately afterwards, and before you know it, you're on a roll. In addition to the obvious benefit of developing partnerships with parents by making this type of phone call, you'll also find these calls beneficial to your emotional state by keeping you from feeling as though you are drowning in some of the more negative aspects of the job. This can easily happen if you spend all your time focusing on the relatively small percentage of students who disproportionately clog up the main office and your inbox with referrals.

In addition to calling parents when there is something positive to report, allow yourself some time to focus on the "good kids." That is, consider calling the parents of students who probably have never made it to your office—class officers, National Honor Society members, and valedictorians and salutatorians. These parents might initially be shocked to receive a phone call from their child's administrator, but they will appreciate that someone other than just a disciplinarian works at their child's school.

We encourage you also to make positive calls to the parents of even your most disruptive students. Regardless of the trouble these students might cause, they have parents who love them. To be inundated with phone call after phone call about all the wrong their child has done must be exhausting, so why not try to find some kind of positive that you can share with parents? In such cases, you might comment that he was cooperative, was not defiant, or didn't argue back; the parents of these students will appreciate something, no matter how little, to get them through a tumultuous year.

Create Small Wins

A quick way to forge a positive rapport with parents is to work with them to achieve small victories. For example, suppose that you receive a complaint from a parent who hasn't heard back from a teacher. Whether she e-mailed a teacher about a grade or called him to ask a question or request information, the parent has yet to receive a timely response from the teacher and, as a result, has shared this concern and frustration with you.

It would certainly be wise to agree with the parent on an issue like this, that she should have heard back from the teacher. You might respond by saying,

"You're right; he should have responded to your e-mail [voicemail] in a timely fashion; that doesn't sound like Mr. Smith." You might then follow up with, "Do you mind if I talk to him about this?" Validating the parent's concern, asking for her permission to take action, and implicitly pledging to do something about the matter will certainly build credibility with her. You might even close the conversation with her by saying, "I will speak to him before the day is over, but could I ask you for a favor? If it isn't too much trouble, can you let me know if you don't hear from him within twenty-four to forty-eight hours?" Again, you are inviting the parent to be a part of the solution while also implicitly vowing to remain involved if the situation is not rectified. Furthermore, asking her to keep you informed serves an even more important purpose: it helps you stay on top of your teachers' actions and know if they are doing what they should be doing.

Keep Promises (and Know What Promises You Can Keep)

Although you can't always give people what they want, you can give them your word, and you should never treat that lightly. A promise is a solemn vow, so you should use care to ensure that you are actually able to make one, in the same way that you might pause before doing so with a family member rather than risk breaking your word with your loved ones. Similarly, don't make a promise to a parent simply because you feel obligated to, feel bad for some reason, feel you owe him, or for some other reason, unless you are sure you can uphold the promise made. If you blindly make a promise and then discover that you cannot keep that commitment, you are damaging yourself and your credibility. If this does happen, you need to be able to follow up with that person and immediately and openly admit you are unable to keep your promise. You can anticipate that he already knows you fell short on your commitment, so now he may be waiting to see if you will acknowledge the shortcoming, which can go some way to restoring his impression of you as a professional.

Speak Parent to Parent

Not every administrator can use this tactic, but you can create a connection with parents by establishing a common ground with them based on your own parenting experiences. If you are seeing misbehavior at school, there is a good chance that the parent is seeing it at home as well. When invited into a dialogue, parents often will confess frustration and exasperation over changes in their child's behavior. Validate their feelings and let them know that they are not alone: that just as they are struggling with their child, you have had struggles with your own children. Remind them that just as you have done, they need to hold the line: it is the student's job to test the boundaries, and it's the parents' job to hold the boundaries firmly in place. You might also offer them any kind of resources that are available to parents, such as support groups or parenting courses.

We've also known parents to ask administrators who don't have their own children what they would do if they did; that is a difficult question to navigate. If you don't have children of your own, you can certainly offer what you know other parents have done or what you might do, but because you cannot truly understand their situation, it can be difficult to offer this kind of advice, and your advice can easily be challenged: "Well, you wouldn't really know because you don't have any children." However, you can still express your understanding and offer sympathy: "I can only imagine how you must be feeling" or "I don't know how you feel, but if I were receiving this information, I'm sure I would be upset, so this must be difficult for you." This kind of statement is hard to challenge and can de-escalate the situation, helping you establish common ground so that you can proceed with the conversation about the issue at hand.

Note Conversations

It is critical that you document your contact with parents, regardless of how well you believe the conversation went. We are not suggesting that you maintain an elaborate log, but rather something simple to help you keep the facts straight. For example, one trick we learned from a principal is to keep a small notebook by our telephone, and as soon as we finish the conversation or leave a voicemail, we immediately record the following information: the date, the time, the person we spoke to (or called), the number dialed, and the topic of the conversation. It is that last part that you can choose to elaborate on with as much or as little information as you want, but what you do have then is a record that you can easily refer to if you ever need the basic details.

Communicate and Enforce Expectations

Parents find it frustrating when schoolwide expectations are not clearly communicated, enforced, or consistent. For example, it might be that teachers are expected to contact parents about missing assignments. However, some teachers may not be aware of this expectation; or all of them are aware of it, but not all are adhering to it. Teacher communication with parents is crucial yet sometimes very easy to omit or, worse yet, circumvent, so you can strengthen your relationship with parents by ensuring that teacher communication takes place.

Another way to foster your partnership is to make sure that you also communicate effectively and often with parents. Even if some parents are not as involved as you would hope, that does not mean that they are disengaged or indifferent. By keeping parents informed, you help ease anxiety, present yourself as sincerely wanting their involvement, and increase the chance of their participating in the life of the school. Although newsletters can still be effective, be sure to explore other means of communicating and connecting with parents, such as e-mail lists, phone-outs, the school's Web site, and social media.

Keep Calm

We realize that it is cliché to say that nothing can be solved by raising your voice, but the reminder is worthwhile: it is all too easy to lose your cool when you are in the middle of an intense conversation, and it takes conscious reminding and self-restraint to refrain from escalating the situation and instead focus on defusing the situation. By that we mean avoiding raising your voice, being argumentative, cutting the parent off, or making sarcastic comments. Rather, if a parent raises her voice, try extra hard to maintain your normal speaking volume and maybe even lower it a notch. Doing so might cause the parent to unconsciously do the same. You might also try folding your hands to remain calm, pleasant, and in control. Maintaining a calm demeanor is important to help "convey respect and dignity. It's easy for well-mannered people to act with respect and dignity when all is going well. The challenge is to convey these attitudes when anger, disagreement, and finger pointing are coming your way. In all interactions with parents, respond to them in the same way you want them to respond to you" (Curwin, Mendler, and Mendler, 2008, p. 199).

INVOLVE PARENTS

Nurturing parental involvement is an important part of being an administrator because, as we have already noted, parents are an important part of the equation that results in student success; as Brooks (2011) writes, "The elevation of family engagement as a key strategy for improving schools is grounded in two decades of research that have demonstrated benefits that are strongly correlated with effective family engagement—higher attendance rates, fewer discipline incidents, and improved achievement" (p. 25). Numerous studies (as well as common sense) confirm this sentiment; as Fiore (2004, p. 184) explains, drawing on data from the National Coalition for Parent Involvement in Education, parent partnerships have multiple positive effects:

- Students do better in school and life.
- Parents become empowered.
- Teacher morale improves.
- Schools get better.
- Communities grow stronger.

These benefits do not arise by accident, and, unfortunately, it seems more difficult to get parents involved as their children reach high school age; they are often less likely to visit the school for events and to remain as involved as they were when their children were in elementary school. Understanding the value of parental involvement, you might need to reach out to your parents in order to develop that partnership.

Enlist Help

People enjoy helping because it satisfies a desire to feel needed and to have a sense of purpose. Even in schools where it is difficult to get parents engaged, if you can find a way to tap into this desire, you can bring them into the building. The key is to determine the parents' strengths and talents and to be open to using them. For example, if parents have to list their place of employment on your students' emergency information cards (and if they don't, you might want to consider adding that as a field), you might review the cards in order to identify some of the parents' skill sets and knowledge areas, and potential resources they might have at their disposal. If your school issues a newsletter to families, you could include a section where you solicit parent help and include a form for parents to mail back that has them list areas in which they feel comfortable helping.

You can also build bridges with parents by harnessing their energy. For example, many parents call regularly with complaints or suggestions about which they are passionate. Working with parents who have complaints can be time consuming if you are unable to bring a focus to it, but if you have parents who offer suggestions or solutions, you would be wise to enlist their help and their ability to research the feasibility of their ideas. For example, perhaps you have a parent who has repeatedly mentioned the lack of an aesthetically pleasing main entrance. Instead of simply nodding your head or referencing an inadequate budget, ask him if he has a suggestion or a solution. He might offer that a rock garden in the front would greatly enhance the curb appeal of the school; now you need to see if you can enlist his help in bringing this to fruition. It's like the old adage: "Don't bring me problems; bring me solutions." You don't want to add more to an already impossibly long laundry list of things you must do and likely do not have the time for. The point is to encourage your parents to bring you proposals for solutions to problems, and empower them by being a partner when possible. And you never know: in our rock garden example, that same parent might know someone who knows someone who is in the landscaping business and willing to help with beautifying the front entrance, or he may know parents who are willing to run a fundraiser for the improvements.

Seek Volunteers

Even though parent involvement seems to taper off in the high school years, many parents still want to be a part of their child's education, especially as she nears her senior year and the end of an era. Tap into those feelings by encouraging and welcoming volunteers in your building. You might suggest that they help chaperone a field trip; provide supervision in the cafeteria; assist in the classroom, clinic, or main office; or serve on a team or committee that has a direct impact on their child. Regardless of what they opt to do, be sure to offer some kind of training with clear expectations and clear direction, and remember to thank them with a handwritten note and even some kind of small token of your appreciation when possible, which could be as simple as a school spirit item with the name of the school on it.

Ask, "Can You Help Me?"

An effective way to invite parents into a partnership is to literally ask for their help. For example, if a student has been sent to your office for misbehaving or some other minor infraction, when you call his parents, you might couch the phone call to them in the following way: "Can you help me by talking with Joe about . . . ?" Whether you do or do not give the student consequences for his misbehavior is not the point. Rather, what you have done is invite the parents to be partners in the solution; they don't feel as helpless as they might when having an outcome dictated to them. And how do most parents respond when you ask them for help with their child? In many instances, we've found that some parents recommend a disciplinary consequence even more stringent than what we were considering. By asking for the parents' help, you open the door for a dialogue about their child, the disciplinary consequences you have at your disposal, and the reason behind them; you also gain an opportunity to brainstorm other solutions.

Invite Parents to School

For some parents, the last time they were in a school might have been when they themselves attended. To make what occurs in the school transparent, invite parents to observe a class (and you might even discuss later with them what they observed). You could also hold open houses so that parents have a chance not just to meet the teachers but also to tour the facility and learn what has changed in schools since they last attended. Or you might host a continental breakfast or coffee on a Saturday morning, inviting parents to drop in and talk with you or the entire administrative team. Last, by inviting parents not simply to join committees or associations (boosters, PTAs, and so forth) but to participate in significant work in the form of school improvement teams, you demonstrate that you value them as partners in their child's education.

Offer Classes

Another way to involve parents in the school is by offering evening classes, workshops, or seminars. For example, you might have a foreign language teacher who is willing to volunteer her time (or maybe there is a way to compensate her) to teach classes for parents. You could also contact outside agencies and see what kinds of workshops they might be able to offer. Or better yet, the parents in the community might be interested in volunteering their time to offer a presentation or to teach some kind of seminar.

Provide Child Care, Translators, and Food

Many parents who want to visit the school for a meeting, event, or open house are sometimes unable to because they have child-care issues. To assist them in this area, you might see if one of the extracurricular service organizations or teachers in your building would be able to help. Some parents might not feel comfortable coming to the school because they are unfamiliar with the American educational system or believe that their level of proficiency with English would hinder their ability to make their time there meaningful. When possible, secure translators in advance from your district or seek the help of staff members to assist these parents. And finally, every parent, regardless of race or creed, enjoys even the simplest of spreads; something as simple as coffee, water, and snacks sets an inviting and hospitable atmosphere for your guests.

KEEP THE FOCUS ON THE STUDENT

In most interactions with parents, keeping the focus on their student is easy. In these circumstances, you and the parent have come to some tacit agreement that the student's needs are your main priority. However, this is not always the case for every exchange you will have with parents. Conversations can quickly and easily move away from the student's needs, so it is important that you find ways to keep the focus on the student and in some cases even respectfully remind the parents that your office is a place of business where you model what you value for your students, which can even include ensuring your students' welfare.

Rely on Students' Explanations

Quite simply, among all the interactions you will have with parents, there will be a very small number of times when they are so upset about the given situation that anything you say only exacerbates it. If in these cases there appears to be a major discrepancy between what they believe and what their child has admittedly done, any frustration directed at you is difficult to overcome, for obvious reasons. In these cases, you might want to consider relying on the student's explanation rather than further antagonizing the parent by protesting more. Instead, have the student explain to his parent what happened; prompt him by saying, "Stan, could you remind us what I said the last time we met about . . . ," or "Remember when we spoke about my expectations concerning . . . ; could you share with us what they are?"

Redirect to the Student's Best Interest

Many times, an upset parent will try to turn the situation involving their student into a situation about you instead. You might have already heard some of these spins—that you are out to get him, that you never liked him, that you don't know what you're doing—and we're confident that you can come up with even more on your own. The focus of their energy is you, not the student or the situation.

Such intense conversations make it difficult to point out the contrary, so rather than engaging in a tit-for-tat, bring the focus back to what is good for their student, explaining that what you are doing is necessary and in the best interest of their child. It is possible they will disagree with that statement or position as well, but it is the best way to depersonalize the conversation as well as to explain why you are doing what you are doing.

Say, "I'm Not Able to Discuss That"

It is natural for parents to want to know what is going to happen to the other student (or teacher, depending on the nature of the situation) who was involved in the situation with their child. In fact, their need for assurance of justice and equity (not to mention your own) is very powerful and can be extremely difficult to deflect. The best response is a pat one. For example, for the parent requesting to know the disciplinary consequences the other child received, you might respond with, "I understand why you are asking, but I can't discuss another student with you, let alone his discipline. Surely you can understand that, as you wouldn't want me discussing your child or his discipline with another parent." Most parents readily understand and can relate to this. If you are met with any push-back, you could certainly follow up by saying, "Let me assure you that I am equitable with my consequences and that I have addressed the other student." The key word there is "equitable." Some parents will want to know if what you did was fair, so we suggest that you use that word specifically: what is fair is not always equitable, but what is equitable is sometimes the fairest thing you can do.

If the issue the parent is asking about concerns a staff member, the same rule applies: there is little you can share with him. The most you should probably say is, "It will be handled in an appropriate manner" or "It is a personnel matter, and I cannot discuss it." You can certainly reassure the parent that the issue will be addressed, and many will still want to know what will happen, but there is a very low level of transparency that you are able to offer here. All you can do is reiterate your feeling on the issue, your commitment to addressing it, and your assurance that appropriate action will be taken.

Say, "Please Don't Speak to Me Like That"

Emotionally intense situations are bound to ruffle feathers. If the conversation becomes heated and inappropriate, you need to establish boundaries. Making it clear that certain behavior or speech is unacceptable is permissible if done professionally. Moreover, you even have an obligation to assert this, and in our experience, doing so often causes the parent to pause and realize that due to the charged situation, a time-out was in everyone's best interest.

For example, you might say something like "Let me stop you right there, Mrs. Smith, because you know me well enough that I would never say that" or "Please don't talk to me like that. I am not raising my voice, and I would appreciate the same respect that I am showing you," or something along those lines. Again, the key is in how you make your statement, and if the behavior or speech does not abate, then you need to make it clear that the conversation cannot continue: "Mrs. Smith, I don't think this is going to be a productive conversation for us, so I suggest that we continue it at another time that would work with your schedule." If you are unable to make any progress and find yourself being verbally abused, then it is appropriate to end the meeting or call. But be sure never to hang up in anger and always give the parent a warning. You might say, "If this continues, I will be forced to hang up," and if it does, simply say, "I'm sorry Mrs. Smith, but I really think I need to end this call now. Thank you." After you have done so, immediately document the date and time of the phone call and capture key elements of the conversation, including what led up to your ending the call.

Protect the Student

Even though the idea of protecting students from abuse is drilled into your head in preparatory programs and county in-services, when you are staring it face-to-face, it is easy to forget your responsibility to report the incident and protect the child. For example, we can recall one incident when we had insisted that a parent had to come in for a meeting with her son. The mother was so irate with her son and his disrespectful attitude that while sitting side by side with him, she turned her body halfway around and swung at him with a closed fist, hitting him in the jaw so hard that he fell out of the chair. The parent then stated, "I just did what I had to do. I know now you're going to do what you have to do, so I will be going." Although this is an extreme example, you are likely to witness behavior and actions that might necessitate a phone call to Child Protective Services, and this event certainly warranted such a call. Keep in mind that a failure to report such an incident can quickly lead you into liability.

The same can be true for verbal abuse, although those situations are a bit fuzzier. You could certainly inject yourself into the conversation and say something like, "We don't talk to children that way here at Kennedy High School." And although we have done that, we have also had parents respond that he is their child and that it is none of our concern. Again, these are slippery situations, so if you find yourself in one, you might explain, "While I understand that you may do that in your home, this is a place of business, so I would appreciate it if you lowered your voice [refrained from using that language]." But when in doubt about a line being crossed with verbal abuse, you should always seek the advice of a supervisor to see if you need to report it.

GO ABOVE AND BEYOND

Parent partnerships don't develop overnight. Even if you do everything we have mentioned and then some, you still may not necessarily succeed in forging a partnership with a particular parent. Sometimes you'll need to go above and beyond the usual. Although not an exhaustive list, the following are a few things you can do to demonstrate that you are interested in forming a partnership with parents and that you value their child. Moreover, by engaging in these kinds of activities, you are indirectly building the foundation for partnerships with your future students' parents.

Call in the Evening

Late after office hours have ended, a local veterinarian makes follow-up calls to his clients from his office. He uses this evening time after the dinner hour to check in on how his patients are faring. His approach has earned him a sterling reputation in the community. He demonstrates care in everything he does, but his evening calls also send the message that he is working late and yet finds the time to check in with his clients, rather than simply leaving voicemails during his office hours when clients are at work and unable to be reached. We urge you to do the same.

Making evening calls is particularly easy to do when you have administrative coverage at night for an athletic game or an extracurricular event. It can be tempting to catch up on other work or to simply decompress until the event starts, but be sure to devote some time beforehand to making follow-up calls to parents. If your parents are working daytime hours, you are not interrupting them at their place of business, and you have also allowed them a little time to settle in and relax after arriving home, both of which can make them a bit more receptive to receiving a phone call from you. If you are concerned about these calls taking too long, start the conversations with something like "I had a little time to make a few phone calls this evening, and wanted to be sure you are one of them." This can help parents understand that you don't have a lot of time but that you are making connecting with them a high priority.

Conduct Home Visits

For a variety of reasons, some parents are difficult to get a hold of. Many administrators might give up, work solely with the student, or write off the student and his family, but we suggest that one way to attempt to make a connection with parents and work in the student's best interest is to visit them at their home. We've both had overwhelmingly positive experiences doing this, even in what some would call difficult communities. We also know of an administrator who adopted the practice of *walking* from house to house on Friday afternoons in the low-income and crime-ridden neighborhood that her elementary school served. And before she had even spoken with a single parent, her visibility was a statement in and of itself: here was an unaccompanied, diminutive woman strolling through a neighborhood where residents themselves were reluctant to do so. And rather than enjoy the first night of her weekend at home, she chose to visit the families of her students. Her visits ingratiated herself to the community and became a fixture of Friday nights in that neighborhood.

Of course, we caution you if you decide to employ this tactic to make sure that you are comfortable with it, because we are not suggesting that you do anything that could endanger your well-being. The potential benefit, though, is enormous as you remind community members of the doctor of old who used to make home visits. If you do decide to try this out, be sure to prepare in advance by organizing folders that contain the students' grades, discipline and attendance records, and contact information, as well as your communication log.

Be Visible

One obvious (and important) form of being visible is to be seen in between classes and before and after school, but here we are referring to community involvement, which can take a number of forms: frequenting local businesses and restaurants within your school's attendance zone to demonstrate that you support the community, and appearing at homeowner association meetings, community events, PTA meetings at the feeder schools, and the like.

The dynamics of the relationship between parent and administrator can be complex and difficult. Although there are certainly some partnerships that are easy to develop because the parents are in need of your help, there are just as many that are rocky and difficult for various reasons. Regardless of the kind of partnership you have with the parents of your students, you and they are already standing on common ground: you share the bond of wanting to see their students succeed. We offer the strategies in this chapter to help you build from that common ground, overcoming obstacles and strengthening these relationships. For if you truly believe and expect the education of your students to be a partnership, remember that the power to create these relationships with their parents is in your hands.

Facilitating Parent Conferences

You have been out of your office the better part of the day. After returning from court, where you were subpoenaed for a student violation from earlier in the marking period, you find yourself covering a class due to a shortage of substitute teachers, reviewing video of a bus incident from the morning run, meeting with a union representative and a teacher, working with the building engineer to fix a leak in the roof and relocating the affected classes, judging a speech contest in an English class, returning yearbook proofs to the sponsor, and meeting with a collaborative team about its benchmark assessment results, you finally sit down to review the testing schedule for the upcoming window of high-stakes assessments. But this moment is short lived as you notice the red light blinking on your phone set. It's a voicemail from Mrs. Britton, a parent with whom you have never previously conversed. Understandably upset, she is calling to schedule a meeting immediately, as she has not heard back from her son's counselor or his teachers regarding his marking period grades. You're familiar with the student: an affable, polite student who has rarely been in trouble. You pull up the student's information in the database and immediately notice a pattern of low grades across select classes over the past two marking periods. As you scan your calendar for an opening, you begin dialing Mrs. Britton.

As a classroom teacher, you probably sat in numerous parent conferences, the majority of them dealing with academic issues. Most likely, though, you didn't see or recognize the nuances, complexities, and dances that often took place during the meetings or that went into their planning. What you did know, however, was that parent conferences could be slippery, and there were probably more than a few instances when you dreaded going to them because of how difficult they could be, whether because of the student, the parents, and maybe even the administrator involved. As an administrator facilitating parent conferences, you've come to appreciate that your role in them is a daunting one: you must be able to support and protect your staff members, maintain or develop the confidence of your parents, and make sure that the student's best interest is being served and her needs met.

Parent conferences are typically held or requested for three main reasons: academic performance, concerns about the classroom teacher's effectiveness, and student misbehavior. These areas are often overlapping or interrelated. The main thing to keep in mind walking into these meetings, and perhaps even when starting these meetings, is that even if all the participants involved disagree about how they got to the table, they should all be able to agree that they are committed to helping the student achieve success. This gives everyone a common thread or common ground from which to proceed.

BEFORE THE CONFERENCE

Successful conferences don't happen by magic. Prior to any kind of parent conference, whether it is with one teacher or every teacher the student has, you will need to prepare in order to increase the chances of its being a meaningful and successful conference.

Talk with Teachers Beforehand

For some parent conferences, it is a good idea to talk with participating teachers in advance. It is wise not only to get a handle on their perceptions of the issues and what they might say but also to determine what kind of rapport they have with the parents and students, and how often they have communicated with the parents prior to the meeting. Inquiring about the student's attendance, behavior, and progress in class and any other anecdotal information they can share with you prior to the conference prevents your being caught off guard during the meeting.

An even more important reason to talk with your teachers prior to a meeting is that you need to strike a balance between showing support for your teachers and supporting your parents' concerns. In some cases, you may want to explain to your teachers that you will not allow things to get out of hand, but there are also rare circumstances in which you will need their coordinated help.

There are different ways you can set up this coordinated effort. For example, develop a pat phrase for your teachers that will signal to them that you are excusing them from the meeting because there are signs of its turning in an unacceptable direction or that you will have limited control and ability to guide the outcome. You might coach them to listen for something like, "Thank you, teachers, for taking the time to come today because I know you have [or have had] a busy day" or "Teachers, I know you need to set up for your next class, so thank you for coming." Statements like these are appropriate for any type of meeting when your teachers are no longer needed in attendance. Under difficult circumstances, however, they serve as helpful cues that it is time for your teachers to leave the room. And unless you signal otherwise, these phrases are definitive, even if the parents protest that they still would like to talk more. You can assure parents with something along the lines that "Mr. Smith is very responsive and can be reached via e-mail, and I will be more than happy to give you his address before we're finished today." The parents may not be aware of your planning efforts, but in a short amount of time they will see you are well prepared to have a productive and focused meeting. Your teachers will appreciate being part of your planning thoroughness.

Determine Meeting Attendance

Although parent conferences may feel the same after a while, every one of them is unique. You will quickly discover that for every parent who wants all his child's teachers present at the meeting, there are a number of parents who actually *don't* want them there. We've even known some who flatly stated, "I just want to talk with you because you're their boss; you can then go figure out how to fix it with them."

When possible, it is ideal to have not only the teachers and parents present but also the student and counselor. In most instances, parents agree that their child should be present, but they sometimes resist the idea. In a high school setting, we respond by saying that it is important for us to have the student know what we are saying; we would be afraid of undoing the trust and the relationship that we have worked so hard to build or that was so tenuous to begin with. We further stress that it is important for the student to hear what we are saying firsthand and that we're curious to hear his perceptions regarding the situation. This is not to say, however, that you should only meet when the student is present. It is perfectly acceptable to talk privately with parents before or after the conference; you just don't want to exclude the student from being part of the process and outcome. It is also important to have the counselor present because she might be privy to different information than the other stakeholders or have a different perspective of the situation.

In middle schools, parents' resistance to including their child is a bit stronger and more common, but the importance of having the child present is no less. Some parents contend that their child does not possess the necessary maturity to be present, that she lacks the ability or maturity to actively problem-solve. An effective response to this argument is that the student needs to have opportunities to develop these skills before she progresses to high school, so what better, safer place than with a group of adults who care about her and have her best interest in mind?

Use Care in Scheduling

Although there are times when last-minute meetings occur, these should be few in number. Respect your teachers and your parents by giving them enough advance notice of the meeting. A general rule of thumb in scheduling them is that teachers should never be pulled out of their classes and away from students in order to attend a parent conference (with some exceptions, such as IEP meetings and the like), and their lunch period should never be infringed on. If the conference is just with one teacher, it should be easy to schedule it around her planning period or even her duty period if you can find coverage for her; however, if the meeting involves all of the student's teachers, it would be difficult to hold it during the school day and not interfere with instructional time. In these instances, holding the conference before school ensures that there is a fixed end time to which you are forced to adhere.

Whether the meeting is before, during, or after school, you might offer the parents a letter of verification stating that they attended a required meeting concerning their child, in case they need evidence for their employer because they will be missing work. This is another way to demonstrate your willingness to assist the parents as an advocate for their child's needs. Please note that if you do generate such a letter, be sure to specify only the date and time of the meeting and not its nature or content.

Prepare Materials

Depending on the purpose of the conference, it is essential that documentation of all aspects of the student's performance be available for the meeting. If you are facilitating a conference that includes teachers, you might want to remind them in advance that they should bring their attendance records, grade reports, a list of missing work, and even their communication log to the meeting. If it would be helpful to have the discipline record or even the cumulative file available, be sure to secure those in advance as well. If teachers are not going to be present at this meeting, make sure you have solicited anecdotal or formal feedback on the student.

Stage the Room

Just as when you are mediating a meeting between students, you want to stage the meeting area for a parent conference. You want to ensure that teachers have clear access to the exit; be sure to seat parents the farthest from the door. Establishing such a setup might not sound important on the surface, but we're sure you can recall a conference that did not go very well, and the awkward silence as you tried to squeeze behind a parent's chair on the way to the door. Also, seating parents opposite the door minimizes the chances of their preventing your teacher from making it to his class; parents may want to talk further about an issue while the teacher is on his way out of the room on your dismissal. It is crucial that you demonstrate respect for your teachers' professional obligations. In addition, if teachers are allowed to be excused from the meeting after sharing their individual concerns and are not required to wait for all the other teachers to have their say, then this type of seating arrangement better facilitates their exit. Be sure to communicate to parents at the beginning of the meeting that teachers will be leaving, so that the parents are not surprised or perplexed when they do.

DURING THE CONFERENCE

Whether you initiated the parent conference, were invited to attend it, or were even summoned at the last minute to report to it, at some point everyone in the room will be looking to you for guidance. Your leadership may be needed in regard to how to proceed next; you may need to take control of the meeting or to ensure that something will actually happen as a result of the meeting—in short, you need to ensure that the conference is facilitated effectively.

Set the Tone

It is important to set a positive, welcoming tone at the start of the conference. Some parents might be carrying the "baggage" of having had their own negative school experiences or are frustrated with their child's current situation in school, so anything you can do to set them at ease is in everyone's best interest. Thank them for coming in, be sure to smile, and try to begin the meeting by stating something specific and genuinely positive about the student, such as, "Maria always makes good decisions," "Denny always demonstrates care for others," or "Denarius's teachers are very appreciative of how helpful he is."

Clarify the Purpose of the Conference

It's helpful to state the purpose of the meeting at the start of it. For example, if you were holding a child study meeting, you might begin by welcoming everyone and simply stating that you are holding an annual child study meeting as indicated in the student's file. However, when possible, ask the stakeholder(s) to clarify the purpose of the meeting. In the case of the child study, you might then ask the parents to specifically explain or describe what their concerns are. In some cases, you might even have the student explain why everyone is gathered. If a teacher initiated the conference, ask him to briefly explain his reason for calling the meeting. You might further add, if necessary, "The purpose for our meeting is unfortunate, a situation that could be difficult to resolve, but I am looking forward to making the best of this as we can by working together."

Regardless of who states the purpose of the conference, it is important to identify it in order to maintain the focus of the meeting, especially if time is limited.

Introduction of Participants

If there is a chance that not everyone seated around the table knows one another, you should definitely explain that you would like the participants to introduce themselves. If you have enough time, you might even make place cards for each member because a parent could potentially be meeting more than seven people for the first time and can very easily forget someone's name. It can set a personable tone if the parent were able to easily recognize and refer to someone by name over the course of the conference. These do not have to be elaborate cards produced on a printer; we've brought in five-by-eight-inch index cards folded in half lengthwise and simply asked each participant to write his or her name on a card so that others can see.

Share Evidence

Even though it might be upsetting for parents to see evidence of a lack of progress, learned skills, or applied effort, it is important to share whatever evidence you have with them that sheds light on the situation. In some cases, presenting a simple grade sheet is not enough; rather, sharing work samples can better illustrate the purpose of the meeting. Without such objective documentation, your teachers (or you) are simply sharing speculations, which the parents could interpret as being subjective.

Solicit Input

Regardless of who has stated the purpose of the meeting, you need to solicit input and feedback from all attendees. For example, if the parent has stated that she is concerned about Johnny's progress during the second marking period, you should ask the student why he thinks he has fared poorly and then ask the teachers about their observations. During this time, you might need to ask clarifying questions of the student and to rephrase and summarize what has been said in order to get to the root cause of the issue. We would suggest that your teachers are familiar with the expectation that parent conferences are forums to help students succeed, not to make them feel worse than they might already; nor do we want the student to feel badgered. The meeting needs to be a supportive one, and although teachers should identify areas where the student needs to improve, they should also be prepared to offer specific praise about the student so that he walks away feeling supported and confident that whatever goal is set is achievable. This approach will help your staff develop a positive relationship not just with the student but also with the parents.

Develop an Action Plan

The purpose of any meeting is not simply to identify problems but also, more important, to develop solutions. At some point near the end of the meeting, you should summarize what the main concerns are and then ask each attendee what can be done to resolve them. After summarizing the concerns, you might ask the student to state what he thinks needs to be done to rectify the situation. Whether he is able to identify a solution or not, you should then ask the teachers as well as the parents what their suggestions are for moving forward. After receiving all this input, restate it again so that everyone is aware of what needs to be done and who will do what. If appropriate, you might want to follow up with an e-mail to the parent, teachers, and, when appropriate, the student, that captures the agreed-on action plan so that everyone is on the same page moving forward. For example, if it were determined that the teachers need to ensure that the student has recorded his assignments in his planner each day and that the parent will check the planner each night, the e-mail sets out the details and serves as a reminder of everyone's responsibility for specific tasks and how they will continue working toward supporting the student's success. Finally, part of the action plan is to set a date to follow up with all parties involved.

Reasons for Ending Meetings

You may not have experienced this yet—and, yes, it is a rare occurrence—but we're confident that at some point, for any number of reasons, one of your meetings will need to end prematurely, or you will need to dismiss your teachers rather abruptly. Even if you employ every technique you can think of, there may come a point when you need to state that the meeting is over and thank the parents for their time.

Establishing boundaries and expectations with your parents can help prevent escalation. Basically, if parents start using obscene language or start escalating attacks (professional, but especially personal), you need to politely remind the parents that they are in a place of business: everyone entering the building is expected to follow the same guidelines that are in place for students because you believe that it is important that you (and the parent) model what you value. But if the parents continue to exhibit the same undesirable behavior, then you have no other recourse but to ask your teachers to leave. Circumstances that might dictate such an action include

- *Abusive language.* This includes aggressive speech and certainly obscene or vulgar language and expressions.
- *Threats.* These do not need to be traditional threats that promise bodily harm, but others that are designed to intimidate: vowing to get someone fired, to have her teaching license pulled, to file a lawsuit, and so on. Once these kinds

of statements have been made, it is very difficult to continue with a civil, productive conversation.

- *Professional and personal attacks.* Parents rarely have firsthand knowledge of what has occurred, so although questions are permissible, repeated scathing accusations and assumptions are not.

- *Abuse of time.* When the discussion is going in circles with no foreseeable resolution in the near future, it is appropriate to excuse your teachers.

- *A need for candor.* There will be times when you will need to be so candid with parents that in order to preserve their dignity, you will want to keep the number of participants to a bare minimum.

The aforementioned guidelines can apply to your teachers as well. The following are some additional difficulties that would obligate you to ask them to leave:

- *Lack of preparedness.* If, even after being notified in advance to do so, teachers arrive without detailed information about the sequence of events leading to the meeting, missing work, up-to-date grades, the parent communication log, and attendance, you are less likely to accomplish what you intended with the conference, so rescheduling might be a better alternative. To simply plow ahead without the most accurate or best information simply to honor the parent's time is actually doing the parent and student a disservice: you won't be able to get to the root cause or to problem-solve as thoroughly as you would like. This kind of situation can be an embarrassing one, so aside from apologizing to the parent, make him aware of why it is so important to reschedule the meeting. And before you do reschedule it, be sure to confer with the teacher that she has prepared the needed information.

- *Confrontational behavior.* Granted, teachers are professionals and need to constantly display a professional demeanor, but they are human too. Perhaps their buttons are pushed or their frustration manifests itself in a confrontational manner, whereas they are ordinarily quite professional.

- *Unsupportable action.* You shouldn't be surprised, but you will be: there will be a time when a teacher makes a claim, statement, or offer that you just cannot support. In these cases, a time-out is probably in order to ensure that your intentions are a match with those of the teacher.

AFTER THE CONFERENCE

As important as a parent conference is, it is only as effective as the resulting action plan, which in turn is only as effective as the follow-up to the conference and action plan. Following up might sound like an obvious next step, but it is often forgotten or simply seen as an optional courtesy. In our view, following up is a critical component of the parent conference because it

- Builds and sustains relationships
- Signals your commitment to continuous improvement
- Demonstrates care and attentiveness to the child's needs
- Determines if the action plan was implemented by all participants as discussed
- Gauges if there has been a positive change
- Provides an opportunity to recognize or celebrate improvement and effort
- Assesses the effectiveness of the action plan

Ideally, you established a follow-up date during the conference; if you didn't, mark a date on your calendar that allows enough time for the implementation of the action plan and to see some effect of it occurring on a consistent basis. In terms of with whom to follow up, it would be best to touch base with all stakeholders involved. Ask the teachers if there has been an improvement in class, meet with the student to see if he feels that anything has changed, and speak with the parents to see if they have noticed anything different at home. If over the course of following up or even checking in a second time you discover that there has been no improvement, then you need to determine if you will proceed with another conference or new interventions, or seek other resources.

Parent conferences are opportunities to simultaneously create or strengthen parent partnerships and provide support for students. Every stakeholder seated in the conference room should have the student's best interest in mind, which is a powerful starting point. It is important to acknowledge, however, that both your parents and teachers attending these conferences are likely to be bringing their anxiety to the meeting. Parents might be anxious about their child's progress and will advocate for what they think is best for her; teachers might be worrying about whether they will be supported by administration and whether parents will be open to hearing their perspective. Negotiating these competing needs and facilitating conferences so that everyone feels supported as you work toward the best interest of the student is a balancing act. It is therefore critical that you carefully plan these meetings in advance: the more attention you pay to detail, the better you can ensure a productive and positive outcome for all involved. That forethought can also help you be more sensitive and responsive to the tenor, flow, and content of the meeting and the needs of all stakeholders present.

Navigating Staff Communication

*Y*ou've known for a week that you have a meeting with Mr. Sanders at the start of the last block. But that knowledge has been little consolation: your stomach has been churning over what you know will be an unpleasant conversation. It's not that you don't get along with Mr. Sanders; actually, you generally find him to be quite amiable, and at times you even like him. However, those feelings are complicated by your experiences with him, in that any kind of dialogue that could be perceived as critical sparks dizzying circumlocutions and tangents. When pressed further, he switches from defensive stratagems to offensive maneuvers. And as if those verbal tactics weren't frustrating enough, his indignation in the face of hard facts has a tendency to get under your skin in a way that no other staff member's behavior can. And if your past history with Mr. Sanders is any predictor, you know that your conversation with him will make its way through the grapevine that afternoon. Moreover, if you don't actively guide this conversation, you know it will end with his walking out of your office without any kind of resolution. But you cannot ignore the voicemail you received from Samantha's mother about Mr. Sanders's new policy of not allowing late work to be turned in for any credit and a snarky remark he made to the student when questioned about his practice.

One of the more difficult and sometimes unsettling aspects of being an administrator is having to contend with potentially unpleasant, challenging, and even explosive interactions with staff members. Thankfully, these conversations are the exception rather than the norm, but they still occur. These "crucial conversations," as Patterson, Grenny, McMillan, and Switzler (2002) suggest, consist of three characteristics: varied opinions, high stakes, and strong emotions. The likelihood of these three factors existing in a conversation between you and certain teachers is high: you work in an administrative or supervisory capacity, and your teachers have strong beliefs, thoughts, and attitudes in regard to their craft and what they believe is best for students, which at times can conflict with your opinion. This dynamic almost ensures that not all conversations are likely to conclude with a warm and fuzzy outcome; rather, there may be agreements to disagree, formal reprimands, or, worse yet, grievances in regard to a decision or directive. These situations can also prove to be tough because depending on how you handle them, they can have far-reaching effects and a profound impact on your leadership and ability to work with staff members.

But sometimes the person sitting across from you is not even the problem; rather, how you choose to handle yourself during these challenging conversations is the more pressing issue. It's a natural feeling to want to "win" in these situations, and it is also difficult to manage your emotions and suppress your true feelings and desires. Tough conversations have the potential to bring out the worst in you, whether that is your wanting to put someone in his place, blame someone else, save face, or worse, so it is important to have a repertoire of skills to help you navigate your way through these interactions.

GUIDE CONVERSATIONS

Although many of your exchanges with staff members will be genial and collegial ones about students, a great lesson, and so on, there will be those other interactions that need to be more than just conversations: they will be focused discussions that need to be guided. These are the intense conversations that could result in conflict or bruised feelings and egos; these are the conversations that cannot be ignored. These have to do with tough issues that have made their way to your office because a situation has surfaced that must be resolved. Whether it is because expectations are not being met, the staff member is either difficult or resistant, or his or her actions are running contrary to the overall direction of the rest of the staff, the situation cannot and will not be resolved without your involvement, and it necessitates a change in behavior. Some of these conversations can be particularly thorny because the staff member might not even realize that his or her behavior, practice, or philosophy is flawed, problematic, offensive, or even damaging.

Both the decisions that are made and the way you handle the meeting are collateral outcomes of this kind of conversation, and knowledge of these have the potential to ripple throughout the building, for better and for worse. So although we are not suggesting that every interaction with a staff member is one that needs to be guided, we do believe that it is important for you to be able to provide guidance and clarity in these conversations (and documentation as necessary) in order to achieve the outcome that is in the best interest of students and that is aligned with your school or district's practices and policies.

In preparing for these difficult conversations, it's helpful to reflect on the following three questions:

1. What do I want for myself from this conversation?

2. What do I want for my staff member from this conversation?

3. What do I want for my other staff members or my students (or both) from this conversation?

Asking these questions of yourself provides you with the focus necessary for engaging in these tough conversations and determining your desired outcome. Your answers will help you keep the conversation focused and on track. In addition, Patterson, Grenny, McMillan, and Switzler (2002) recommend asking yourself reflective questions "when you find yourself slipping out of dialogue" (p. 34) during the actual conversation, in order to help restore focus during particularly intense moments.

When actively engaged in conversation with staff members, we have found that relying on the following components can be extremely useful in guiding the dialogue:

- Establish a foundation

- Ask purposeful questions

- Redirect the focus

- Make commitments

- Employ simultaneous monitoring

- Accept the conflict

- Stay rational

- Don't be afraid to apologize

Although all of these components are important, the order in which they arise in the conversation is not. Depending on the conversation and situation, you might find yourself revisiting them throughout the discussion.

Establish a Foundation

In both its literal and its figurative sense, a foundation provides support for a structure to be built upon, or serves as a solid common ground on which to build. When you are guiding a difficult conversation, establishing a foundation with the other person will better enable you to reach your desired outcomes. The following are some strategies for setting this foundation.

Set the Tone   Just as we mentioned in the chapter on parent conferences, it is important to set the tone of the meeting at the very beginning. Even for particularly difficult conversations, it is critical that you demonstrate your professionalism, so be sure to thank your staff member for coming, for spending her time, and so on. Part of setting the tone is also stating the purpose for your conversation; as Abrams (2009, p. 65) puts it, "If this is a serious matter that may involve the person losing this job, say so. If your concern should be considered just 'food for thought' and the listener does not need to undertake any major action, say so." Stating the purpose focuses and guides the conversation; further, ensuring that your staff member understands the purpose of the conversation is simply a matter of fairness on your part.

Acknowledge the Staff Member's Feelings   Simply being in your office can be a stress-inducing or anxiety-laden experience for your staff member. It is important that you understand this and acknowledge this confluence of feelings. Even if your staff member is in the wrong, acknowledging his feelings—frustration, fear, anxiety, and so on—is not the same as conceding to him or condoning unacceptable behavior. Acknowledging his feelings helps disarm him, defuse the situation, and establish empathy. And because his feelings are real, your acknowledging them helps your staff member feel more like a person and less like your employee.

Identify a Goal   Early on in the conversation, ask your staff member what she would like to see accomplished as a result of the conversation. This question can be helpful for getting her to stop and think for a minute, because before she can answer your question, she has to identify the answer for herself. Asking such a question demonstrates that you are willing to listen to her, invites her into the conversation as a partner, and gives her an opportunity to share her thinking about her expectations of you and the conversation.

Demonstrate Respect   Respect is shown and given in many ways, but probably the best way you can do it is simply by listening to the other person and assuring him that he has your full attention. You can also demonstrate respect by practicing active listening techniques, such as clarifying, summarizing, restating, and asking if you accurately understand. When appropriate, it is also important to show empathy; if the situation precludes that, you can certainly express a desire to understand your staff member's point of view. If you cannot establish mutual respect with him or if he loses respect for you, you are likely to struggle with respect issues from others who respect that staff member.

Ask Purposeful Questions

Obviously enough, questions are an essential part of a healthy dialogue. They allow you to clarify an issue, gather information, check for understanding, and keep the dialogue flowing. These are doubly important for our context, but we are specifically referring to what we call *purposeful questions*. These are not simple inquiries but more of a focused probe in order to help you better understand the root issue and the position the other person is maintaining, and perhaps to illustrate that there are better alternatives available to her. These kinds of questions open up and guide the conversation. By peeling back the layers, these questions get the other person to articulate her position or what she was trying to accomplish and help you guide her into the issue from a more reflective perspective and ideally toward a pedagogical epiphany; they can at least cause her to be receptive to reworking her practice. The questions listed are instructive even if you don't need to ask all of them.

Opening Questions

- Can you help me understand why you think this [the practice or issue at hand] is appropriate?

- Could you tell me more about . . . ?

- Could you walk me through your thought process in deciding to . . . ?

- Could you explain to me why you decided to . . . ?

Delving Questions

- Have you known other people who have experienced success with this?
- What evidence tells you that this is [would be] successful?
- How do you know this is effective?
- Could you share with me the other options you considered?
- Why did you choose the option that you did?
- Has it been successful in the past?
- How is it working out for you?

Closing Questions

- What could you do differently instead?
- What might be more effective [efficient]?
- You know I want to support your efforts and practice, but if you're challenged by the [student, parent, school board], how do you suggest that I support you on . . . ?
- If . . . became public, would you be comfortable with how it could be perceived on the evening news?
- Are you willing to reevaluate your approach and take a different one?
- How about touching base after you try that and letting me know how it went?

Helping your staff member learn to reflect may reduce possible resentment or digging in of heels. For example, if you simply say, "This is wrong because . . . ," "Or I can't support this because . . . ," or "I can't believe that you are doing . . . ," you will quickly discover that you will not have many fruitful conversations with your staff. These kinds of statements are challenging, threatening, and confrontational; they are possibly even demeaning and damaging, especially if the staff member was acting in earnest. Making these kinds of statements shuts down both the conversation and the person.

In some instances, the staff member might indicate that she understands what the problem is, but you see obvious signs that it is still not entirely clear to her. When this happens, you will need to explicitly state what she needs to do rather than having her take charge of her own professional growth.

Redirect the Focus

As an administrator, you will often experience the need to redirect the focus of the conversation—that is, to change the course or direction of the conversation if you want to achieve a desirable outcome. We offer some reasons here for a need to redirect the focus, but we're confident that you can come up with some of your own examples.

Negativity   When you are having a conversation with a staff member, your perception may be that the person is merely being negative. Rarely will the other person agree that he is being negative; as far as he's concerned, he is simply expressing his belief or position to you. But you know negativity when you see it: cynicism, skepticism, pessimism, criticisms or complaints about something over which he doesn't even have control or influence, or fixation on the "if onlys." The negativity might even be justifiable. Regardless of what form it takes, though, if the conversation continues in that vein, it will cease to be a productive one: negativity is a barrier that prevents people from finding solutions.

In dealing with these kinds of conversations, you can't immediately redirect the focus. It is important for you first to listen—maybe not to every complaint, but you need at least to demonstrate a willingness to listen, both as a sign of respect and because your redirection of the discussion is going to require that he listen to you. But at an appropriate time, you need to begin redirecting the focus by saying something along the lines of, "You know, I certainly hear what you're saying, but I'm concerned that it isn't going to help us find a solution." This is your launching point to getting the conversation back in a positive direction. You then need to maintain the focus on what can be done, on viable solutions, and on more favorable outcomes.

Tangents   Some people go off on tangents deliberately in order to obfuscate the focus of the conversation or to prevent an outcome that might require a change in their behavior or practice, but there are many others who do not even realize that they are sidetracking the conversation (and whose conversations thus rarely seem to yield results). In these instances, the person is going off in too many directions, and the focus of the conversation is easily lost. The person has made a verbal left turn, and you need to bring her back on track.

In addition to assisting with focusing the conversation, you can take the opportunity to help her learn about her counterproductive behavior (if you do it tactfully); there is a good chance that if you're seeing the behavior in your office, then it is also occurring in meetings and possibly in the classroom as well. A direct approach in these situations is best, so you might say something like, "I'm failing to see the connection between what you're focusing on now and what prompted this conversation, so let's bring the discussion back to the main issue, which is . . ."

Wrong Focus Some people tend to focus on the wrong thing. Sometimes staff members focus more on what is good for them rather than on the overall good, whether that good is for a student, a team, a department, or even the school. In other instances, a staff member's vision might be too narrow, and he is unable to see the "big picture." So the difficult part is getting him to see the world that exists outside his particular sphere.

Our notion of the wrong focus is not limited just to something negative; sometimes staff members focus their effort or attention on a worthwhile issue, but it is not the issue that currently needs addressing. Regardless of the situation, many of these instances are marked by a focus on such specific topics that it is difficult to provide an easy redirection, but a general rule of thumb is to try to redirect the conversation to the values, beliefs, mission, or vision of the school. For example, you might redirect to what is in the best interest of students by simply asking, "How is this going to increase student learning?" if it were an instructional issue, or by stating, "I don't see how this will help your team achieve its goals," and so on.

Make Commitments

Large or small, a commitment on the part of staff members is your ultimate goal in guiding conversations with them. There must be a product or behavioral outcome. If you are having a conversation with a staff member and are not planning on guiding that person to a commitment that she or you have identified (and one that you want or that you can support), then you have to ask yourself, why are you having the conversation in the first place? If there is no goal of making a commitment, the purpose of the conversation, then, is merely to hear each other's position or to tell your staff member how you feel about something she is doing. These are casual or diluted dialogues that at best culminate in weak suggestions that staff members can choose to take or ignore if they like. You shouldn't expect much to change if that is the case.

Instead, there must be firm closure to your focused discussions. This closure takes the form of the staff member's committing to changing a specific behavior (as opposed to an attitude, which will we address in the next section). But a simple commitment is not enough: it is essential that the staff member outline how he will make his changes. Because one of your implicit responsibilities is to help set your staff up for success, having him lay out a detailed plan or helping him do so is a way for you to provide him with the support necessary to be successful with his new commitment. Your responsibility, then, is to help your staff member maintain his commitments, which can be done by seeking his buy-in, following up with him about the status of his commitment, and then documenting his progress (or lack thereof) if necessary.

Seek Buy-In   Part of guiding conversations is identifying in advance, before you even have the conversation, what you would like to see as an outcome or commitment. However, if you ask your staff member for her input on the outcome, you have a greater chance of securing her buy-in. If you simply dictate a resolution to a person (although there are times when doing so is necessary), the lack of buy-in will most likely doom it to failure. So as much as possible, you want to help draw a solution out of the other person so that she owns it and feels empowered to make modifications as necessary to carry out the solution. But you must also keep an open mind to what she suggests, or else you run the risk of appearing to steer or manipulate every conversation to your own desired outcome. If the other person suggests untenable solutions, you need to have one to offer as either an example or as the actual solution. Another aspect of gaining buy-in is identifying a time when you will revisit your discussion and commitment with your staff member.

Follow Up   Depending on the nature of the conversation, you should plan to follow up with your staff member at some point, in order either to assess the efficacy of the change or, in some cases, to determine whether the change was made at all. Let your staff member know in advance that you will be following up with him, as that can help move the verbal commitment into the realm of an actual behavior. By following up with him, you are demonstrating a willingness to measure the effectiveness of what he had committed to and an openness to hearing his input based on his experience with implementing the change. This is also a perfect time to offer congratulations or praise, which can further solidify buy-in. If you neglect to follow up with the staff member, you are unknowingly sending some undesirable messages to your staff. First, you are unconsciously telling the individual that there are more pressing priorities that prevent you from considering his efforts as important for follow-up. Second, you are inadvertently modeling behavior (lack of follow-through) that you wouldn't accept from your staff members themselves. Last, if you never follow up with your staff member, you decrease his motivation to change; consequently, you will find yourself in meetings where people more easily make commitments, and large ones at that, because they know there won't be any follow-up.

Document It is important to keep an informal and sometimes even a formal record of these conversations so that you can easily and accurately reference the details in the future. At the very least, you should create an anecdotal note immediately after the conversation while it is still fresh in your mind; be sure to include the date, the time, the names of who attended the meeting, and brief talking points from the conversation. A higher level of documentation might be a short e-mail to your staff member thanking her for the time she spent with you discussing the issue and how you look forward to talking with her again in the future about whatever change has been agreed on or made. If a very high level of documentation is needed, you would want to capture the facts of the conversation and the agreed-on or stated commitment or expectations in a memorandum. If you choose to document your conversation in writing, we suggest that you let the staff member know in advance as a professional courtesy. Doing so will prevent her feeling that she has been blindsided—that unbeknownst to her, her verbal conversation has "escalated" to being a documented one. Informing her of your intention and having some record of the conversation also raise the level of commitment to follow-through on your part; in essence, once you share a plan of action with someone, you increase the probability of your carrying it out.

Employ Simultaneous Monitoring

A critical component of effectively guiding tough conversations is being able to simultaneously monitor your behaviors, your staff member's behaviors, and the content of the conversation. That is no simple endeavor. Although most of us are able to monitor the content, it is all too easy in a difficult conversation to become blind to behaviors because we are so deeply invested (or entrenched) in conveying our position. Similarly, the staff member's intensity or emotions can also blind you to your own behaviors. You can lose contact with the reality of the conversation, which in turn jeopardizes your ability to guide it to the desired outcome. If you can notice and understand several specific signals simultaneously, you will be better able to guide the conversation:

- *Eye contact.* Direct eye contact conveys interest and attention (although prolonged eye contact can be perceived as intimidating). A lack of eye contact, in contrast, can indicate disinterest and unease and that the message is not getting through.

- *Gestures.* Beyond the obvious pointing of fingers or slamming of the hand on the table, hand movements can be very telling. For example, "running the hands through the hair or rubbing the back of the neck . . . transmit[s] frustration" (Griffin, 1998, p. 179). Moving your hands across your face or mouth can suggest dishonesty, whereas hand-wringing or fidgeting is a sign of anxiety (pp. 28, 178).

- *Posture.* How a person is seated or standing during a conversation is just as revealing as his facial expressions. Whereas sitting upright can convey confidence and attention, slouching in the seat can communicate not only indifference but also defeat—and there *is* a difference between compliance and commitment as opposed to defeat. Folded arms make an even larger statement: they "[indicate] a closed mind or resistance" (Griffin, 1998, p. 179). Finally, leg-shaking or tapping of the feet can indicate irritation or "a desire to be elsewhere, to get away" (p. 179).

- *Facial expressions.* There are those who say that one's facial expressions can be quite accurate and informative in mirroring one's emotional state. For example, "raised eyebrows suggests disbelief" and "narrowing of the eyes communicates disagreement, resentment, anger, or disapproval" (Griffin, 1998, p. 27). A lowered chin "conveys defensiveness or insecurity" and "peering over the top of your eyeglasses suggests doubt and disbelief" (p. 27).

- *Discrepancies.* There should not be a difference between what is actually said and what one's body language communicates. Both the content and the behavior should run parallel to each other.

- *Paralinguistics.* This area is concerned with the manner of speaking, or *how* words are actually said. The volume, pitch, intonation, and inflection of one's speech can both create and greatly alter meaning.

- *Proximity.* Regardless of the space designated for the conversation, your personal space can change. For example, if your space is reduced by participants leaning in, that usually signifies agreement and attention. On the contrary, if participants lean back and create space between them, the literal divide can also be seen as a figurative one.

- *Silence.* If only one person is talking for an extended period of time, it ceases to be a conversation.

If your staff member exhibits any of these indicators, then you need to find a way to redirect the conversation or even offer to take a quick time-out to regroup. If you notice that you are displaying some of these behaviors, then you need not only to regroup your own behaviors but also to try to listen intently while mentally coming back to the three questions (listed earlier) about what it is you want from the conversation and how you are willing to accomplish it.

Another technique we've found helpful when we simultaneously monitor and recognize that the conversation is in trouble is to "go to the balcony" (Ury, 1993, p. 38) to prevent ourselves from reacting impulsively or emotionally. Using this technique, you pretend that your conversation is occurring on a stage; when you are in the midst of a challenging moment, you should imagine climbing onto a balcony that overlooks the stage. From the balcony, you can truly observe what is going on and distance "yourself from your natural impulses and emotions" (p. 38). According to Ury, "The 'balcony' is a metaphor for a mental attitude of detachment. From the balcony you can calmly evaluate the conflict almost as if you were a third party. You can think constructively for both sides and look for a mutually satisfactory way to resolve the problem" (p. 38).

Accept the Conflict

Some administrators are uncomfortable engaging in conflict. However, persuasion and pleading rarely do the trick, so you need to accept the notion that you are bound to engage in conflict with some of your staff members. In fact, DuFour, DuFour, Eaker, and Many (2006) state that "when educational leaders at the district or school level avoid confrontation because they favor keeping the peace over productive conflict, they can do tremendous damage to any improvement process" (p. 172).

Part of accepting conflict is being willing to use strong language. Some leaders use weak language because they think it helps them avoid conflict while still conveying their intention. The problem is that this tactic rarely works. When you speak vaguely, you leave the door open for misinterpretation and for the staff member to either take or leave the recommendation. For example, instead of suggesting that your staff member "should" or "might" do something, you need instead to state your recommendation in clear, strong terms: "The expectation is that you will . . . ," and so on.

Stay Rational

When you are meeting with a staff member, there might be times when he will deliberately provoke you in order to pull you off topic and to diminish your credibility (especially if someone else is witness to the conversation). The best move you can make is to remain calm and rational regardless of what is said or insinuated (along the lines of the chair comparison we referenced at the end of Chapter Three), and at times this means suppressing your urge to lash back. To do anything less, to respond emotionally and viscerally, would only damage your credibility and your ability to make inroads.

Don't Be Afraid to Apologize

We've worked with many leaders who were afraid to apologize because they didn't want to appear weak or unknowledgeable; or if they did apologize, it was often insincere or for the wrong things. An apology can be a powerful tool if it is not seen as manipulation and if you are able to admit to yourself that you are wrong or made a mistake; "leaders who acknowledge errors demonstrate humility and the fact that they are able and willing to grow and learn from their mistakes" (Gabriel and Farmer, 2009, p. 14). An apology can be a crucial action to help keep the conversation flowing; as Patterson, Grenny, McMillan, and Switzler (2002) put it, "you have to give up saving face, being right, or winning in order to focus on what you *really* want. You have to sacrifice a bit of your ego by admitting your error. But like many sacrifices, when you give up something you value, you're rewarded with something even more valuable—healthy dialogue and better results" (p. 76). Equally important, being willing to apologize helps create a safe environment for staff members to apologize as well; it also builds trust with your staff members, and models your expectations of professional behavior.

Convey sincerity in your apology by specifically identifying what it is you are apologizing for and why. Demonstrate empathy by describing how your staff member probably felt and see if there is anything else she wishes to add. But most important, you need to pledge to her not to repeat the behavior that triggered your apology. However, you can't stop at that: you need then to personally commit to changing that behavior. A failure to do so will ultimately reduce your credibility because "an apology isn't really an apology unless you experience a change in your heart" (Patterson, Grenny, McMillan, and Switzler, 2002, p. 74)— or in your behaviors.

FOCUS ON BEHAVIORS, NOT ATTITUDES

Regardless of how effective your school is, you are likely to have interactions with resistant and difficult staff members. These are people who seem to have negative attitudes or rigid mind-sets. They seem to always resist change when it is imperative that they accept it; they undermine improvement efforts, openly challenge authority, and seem to purposely provoke whenever given the chance. Difficult and resistant people act the way they do for a variety of reasons, including the following:

- *Misunderstanding.* There has been a breakdown in communication. A seemingly compliant or easygoing person is missing some critical information and reacts in a way he might not ordinarily.

- *Self-interest.* The staff member is comfortable with her present situation and, as a result, doesn't want to entertain change and will actively fight against it.

- *Fear of change.* Change can disrupt routines and yield unpredictable results, which some people find disturbing.

- *Professional disagreement.* There is a genuine disagreement (not a fabricated one as a result of the previous two reasons) about what should be done.

- *Stress.* Life just seems more complicated and frenetic now, so something new at work can often be the final straw because of the stress (and added or different work) that it will seemingly create.

Regardless of the reason for a staff member's negative attitude and unwillingness to change his mind, you can very easily find yourself exasperated. A natural reaction is to want to change this person's mind or to change his attitude (or even fix him). So you invest a great deal of time and energy presenting information and evidence in an attempt to persuade him, to change his mind.

This is not an inherently wrong tactic, but sometimes you will find that attempting to change an attitude can feel like trying to nail Jell-O to a wall: it seems impossible.

Changing a staff member's mind, or attitude, is difficult to accomplish because an attitude is internal and personal: it is hers—it belongs to her. Given that, as Evans (2010) suggests, teachers tend to prefer stability and continuity, if your discussion with a staff member is centered on the need for change, she is likely to become more entrenched in her thoughts or attitudes because she has control over them. So if the goal of your conversation is to change that person's beliefs, you are likely to fail; you are powerless to impose that kind of change, to demand that she think differently about something. Therefore, if the "ultimate aim is a change in beliefs and assumptions, which cannot be imposed, one must often insist on a change in behavior, which can" (p. 48). As Table 7.1 indicates, there is a noticeable difference between attitudes and behaviors.

Reviewing the table, you might conclude that the issue of attitudes and behaviors is inconclusive and confusing because it calls up a chicken-and-egg argument: Which come first? According to recent research in relevant fields of study (cited by DuFour, DuFour, Eaker, and Many, 2006), "changes in attitudes follow, rather than precede, changes in behavior" (p. 174). These authors explain that "when work is designed to require people to *act* in new ways, the possibility of new experiences are created for them" (p. 174).

Table 7.1
Attitudes Versus Behaviors

Attitudes	Behaviors
Internal	External
A person's feelings or beliefs	A person's actions
Approval or disapproval	Conduct and responses
Difficult to measure	Observable
More subjective, based on perception	More objective, based on concrete information
Not easily changed	More malleable

For example, you might be engaged in a conversation with a teacher about his belief that homework should never be accepted late. After several attempts at persuading him with citations of research and scholarly articles that his mind-set is flawed, you have made no progress: he still clings to his belief and policy of not accepting late homework. In this situation, you need to alter the environment: you no longer attempt to change his view on his policy. Instead, you require that his behavior must now change: he will accept late work. Your hope is that perhaps after he has spent enough time engaging in this new behavior, his attitude might change as he sees that more students are actually turning in their work and demonstrating greater proficiency. In other words, "if you can change people's behavior in desired ways, their attitudes will shift to support the new behavior. This occurs because people feel a strong need to preserve consistency between their behavior and their beliefs. The implication for persuasion is clear: It often makes sense to focus on getting people to act in new ways" (Watkins, 2003, pp. 198–199).

TEND THE GRAPEVINE

You've probably heard the 1960s song "I Heard It Through the Grapevine." The protagonist learns about the imminent end of his romantic relationship, not directly from his girlfriend, but through informal means or other channels. In essence, that is what the grapevine is: a swift informal channel of communication that is fueled by gossip and rumor. And just as an actual grapevine spreads randomly and covers a large area, so does the grapevine at your school.

When we talk of the grapevine, we are not suggesting that educators are busybodies. Like most professionals, educators are apt to engage in shoptalk, or "teacher talk," which is one way they become attached to the grapevine; the fact is, the grapevine thrives in nearly every organization because it "is as permanent as humanity" (Davis, 1988, p. 289). There are no doubt many different reasons why the grapevine exists in your school; it could be that formal communication is poor, that there are some people who like to feel important and be the center of attention, that staff members need an outlet for stress relief, or that it simply satisfies the human urge to interact and make sense of one's surroundings. Regardless of the reasons for it, the grapevine exists in your school; there is very little you can do about it. You should not ignore it but instead analyze it and "consciously try to influence it" (Davis, 1988, p. 289).

Feed the Grapevine

One way to tend the grapevine is to feed it—to purposefully provide it with information that you want flowing to the faculty through informal means. Your efforts will be more effective if you understand how the grapevine operates. Davis (1988) identifies four ways:

- The single-strand chain—Person A tells B, who in turn tells C, and so on.
- The gossip chain—Person A tells everyone he or she comes in contact with or seeks out.
- The probability chain—Person A randomly tells D, who in turn has random contact with B.
- The cluster chain—Person A tells a few people he or she is close to, who in turn tell a few others in their social or professional network.

So, for example, you might take advantage of the gossip chain by deliberately sharing certain information in order to get more truth into the system and dispel rumors. Or you might purposefully even try to have someone "overhear" a conversation. Basically, you are attempting to feed the grapevine with clear, timely, and accurate information. In other instances, rather than formally presenting a new idea to the faculty, you might employ the cluster chain and casually mention the idea in order to test the waters among some key players to help you decide whether it should be rolled out.

Tap the Grapevine

In his studies, Davis (1988) found that 80 percent of rumors circulating through the grapevine were true, so it can be dangerous and foolhardy to simply dismiss the grapevine as mere gossip and not put any stock in its information. An effective administrator understands that it is necessary from time to time to tap into the information available through the grapevine as a way of measuring the climate and morale of the building. You do this by building trust with one or more reliable sources and having informal conversations about information that they hear through the grapevine and that is not being brought to your office. For example, you might discover that the faculty is dissatisfied with the way that student misbehavior is addressed in the office, that some staff members are unhappy that some of their colleagues are not being confronted for not adhering to certain expectations, or that there is a general feeling that faculty meetings are a waste of time. You might even discover who is unhappy and looking for a job somewhere else.

Regardless of what you learn, the point is that you are not acquiring information for information's sake: what you discover should be addressed. You can't confront people in order to confirm what is being spread through the grapevine, nor should you reveal any sources of your information; either of these approaches would result in diminished respect for you and would close off that source of information by potentially burning the person who trusted you. However, there is still a lot you can do with the information you are able to obtain. For example, you could include these items in periodic or year-end opinion surveys and then share the results—and your plan of action—with the staff. You could also address items through either a shared leadership team or a faculty advisory committee (which we encourage schools to implement; see Gabriel and Farmer, 2009). In these meetings, team members could discuss and investigate issues being spread through the grapevine and how they might be resolved.

As you can see, there is a lot to consider when navigating staff communication. Often when we enter these dialogues, "We start out with the goal of resolving a problem, but as soon as someone raises the red flag of inaccuracy or challenges our correctness, we switch purposes in a heartbeat" (Patterson, Grenny, McMillan, Switzler, 2002, p. 36), and we are pulled into a different kind of conversation, one in which we want to prove we are right and to win. So guiding conversations is also about monitoring ourselves and maintaining our own focus.

To assist you in these difficult conversations, you might find it helpful to mentally rehearse the interaction and possible scenarios in order to get a better handle on how the conversation will transpire. Developing potential responses; brainstorming possible solutions; anticipating what the other person might say, argue, or present; and being able to counter or validate and support them depending on the situation and the desired outcome can help you sidestep land mines later. By engaging in some mental preparation and prediction, you lessen the chance of being victimized by the conversation and instead increase the possibility of being able to navigate it successfully.

Chapter EIGHT

Building Capacity

*A*fter *attending two collaborative team meetings, you were able to dedicate the better part of the day to observing teachers and conducting four classroom observations across the different departments that you supervise as well as complete several walkthroughs. As you slide the walkthrough forms into the teachers' mail-boxes, you have already mentally composed how you will structure the postconferences for the formal observations.*

As confident as you are with the different strategies you will employ for each conversation, you can't help but notice that there are common patterns running through the observations and walkthroughs that you conducted. For example, there are practices and behaviors occurring that surprised you on some level because you assumed that the staff were aware that they should shy away from those strategies and habits. Similarly, you didn't see some things occurring both in meetings and in classrooms that you had taken for granted as things that should be happening. As you exit the mailroom, you wonder how this could be the case—you noted the absence of certain practices and items even though you've come across them in professional literature, which you have even referenced during postobservation and evaluation conferences. Certainly there is another way to make these ideas and practices stick?

A challenging—yet very rewarding—aspect of being a school administrator is that in between all the crises that arise and the fires that you must extinguish, you are also expected to improve your teachers' professional practices and develop their leadership skills, a difficult charge indeed for even the most experienced administrator. And as adept as you might be in pinpointing areas needing improvement during a classroom observation or in completing evaluations in a timely manner, these isolated actions most likely will not result in a sustained increase in student achievement or teacher efficacy. Therefore, if you hope to improve the level of achievement in your school, the most viable method is to work with your teachers and invest in "their continuous development" (Fullan, 2008, p. 57). This notion, commonly referred to as building capacity, "concerns competencies, resources, and motivation. Individuals and groups are high in capacity if they possess and continue to develop knowledge and skills, if they attract and use resources . . . and if they are committed to putting in the energy to get important things done *collectively* and *continuously* (ever learning)" (p. 57). It is in this area—of developing teachers' knowledge, skills, and practices—that you have the greatest chance of having a positive impact on the students in your school, which, after all, is the main reason you entered administration: to improve teaching and learning for all staff and students.

MAINTAIN A FOCUS ON DEEP LEARNING

We are unfamiliar with any school that does not engage in some amount of professional development. In most instances, professional development is accomplished through in-service days, primarily when teachers return from their summer vacation to spend some portion of the lead-up to the opening of school by attending mandatory district or school workshops. Many of these sessions are beneficial, but just as many of them are time killers. But even the helpful ones can lose their value if there is only a one-time focus on the topic that was presented, and that is all too often the case. Unfortunately, professional development in schools frequently functions as inoculation: teachers receive their annual booster shot before being sent into their classrooms, and no second thought is given to their professional health until their next annual checkup the following summer. These one-time events cannot be relied on to increase teacher capacity nor to improve student achievement. So if you hope to improve the "wellness" of your teachers or to build their capacity, you need to maintain a focus on professional development throughout the year.

Solicit Input for Professional Development

The first step in building capacity among your staff is determining the actual areas of need. Rather than just offering scattershot staff development that has roots in various places, you ask your teachers to identify their areas of needs and their deficits. One way to do this is to formally survey them about instructional or leadership areas in which they need help. Using this approach, you have a greater chance of gaining buy-in among your staff because they are driving (and owning) the agenda for professional development. For example, you might pose questions in the form of statements in a Likert scale, asking your teachers to rate their knowledge or comfort with such items as instruction (differentiation, reaching second language learners, literacy, and so on), identifying essential skills, assessment (formative, summative), and providing additional time and support to help struggling learners or to enrich advanced learners. The following are examples of scales you might have your teachers use to assess themselves and their teams:

Statement about self:

I differentiate instruction in order to meet the needs of my students.

Strongly Agree	Agree	No Opinion	Disagree	Strongly Disagree
1	2	3	4	5

Statement about your team:

My team members differentiate instruction in order to meet the needs of their students.

Strongly Agree	Agree	No Opinion	Disagree	Strongly Disagree
1	2	3	4	5

These kinds of survey questions can help you determine patterns of need and patterns in what your teachers believe their needs to be. In some cases, you might be surprised by what teachers are willing to admit.

We advise against crafting multipart statements, which can lead to confusion and to skewed responses. Instead, you would be better served to break a multipart statement into separate and distinct statements. For example, rather than presenting the statement "I differentiate instruction in order to meet the needs of my students, and my team members differentiate instruction as well," you should instead present it as two different statements. By doing so, you are able to draw on the results and review data for two different yet related sentiments.

Including statements about individuals as well as about teams can help surface inconsistencies in purported practices. For example, if teachers answer one way in regard to their own practices and another in regard to their team members'

Table 8.1
Survey Results (Tabular Form)

Statement	Strongly Agree	Agree	No Opinion	Disagree	Strongly Disagree
I differentiate instruction in order to meet the needs of my students.	7	6	4	42	27
My team members differentiate instruction in order to meet the needs of their students.	4	5	9	46	22

practices, these data indicate an obvious disconnect. In our own buildings, we would have a follow-up conversation with individual staff members, teams, or in some cases the entire faculty about discrepancies in the responses. Obviously we would never share how individual teachers responded, but we would share the overall results in an effort to determine the cause of the inconsistency.

When you are reviewing needs assessment data as an administrative team or even with the faculty, we strongly encourage you to graph results: you can interpret them at a glance. Although a table sometimes presents a clear picture of the data, a graph or chart often gives you a quicker and easier glimpse into the data. In our example, eighty-six staff members completed a survey; the same results data are presented in Table 8.1 and in graphical form in Figure 8.1.

Most spreadsheet software applications allow you to create graphs of the data; your school district may provide software, and you can also access a free online survey tool, such as Google Docs (http://docs.google.com), which includes spreadsheet data imports and graphs.

Although the graph in Figure 8.1 cannot tell you *why* staff members are not differentiating instruction, you do know that for the most part they are not doing it. These data can serve as some evidence, produced by your staff, as to why you will be offering professional development on differentiating instruction.

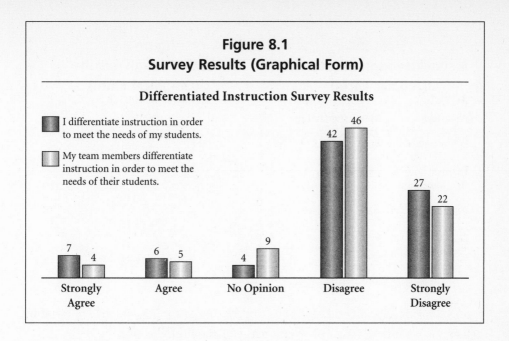

Figure 8.1
Survey Results (Graphical Form)

Differentiated Instruction Survey Results

■ I differentiate instruction in order to meet the needs of my students.

▨ My team members differentiate instruction in order to meet the needs of their students.

Prescribe Professional Development

Another way to build capacity among your teachers is to prescribe, without seeking their input, the professional development that will occur, which is certainly your prerogative. This option is much more diagnostic and prescriptive, which is why some bristle at its authoritative nature, but one could argue that it is necessary because sometimes "providing quality professional learning requires a shift from conducting a needs assessment to determine what educators want to learn to identifying the skills they need to learn to meet identified areas of student need" (Munger and von Frank, 2010, p. 41). In other words, although seeking teachers' opinions on topics about which they would like to learn more is certainly collegial and appreciated by staff, it is not always the most effective way to pinpoint actual areas of need, as their perspective might differ greatly from yours and from what is in the best interest of students.

Your decision to conduct professional development might be based on your school district's or school's needs, such as when you are implementing new technology or software applications. In other instances, the professional development being offered is based on specific teacher-level needs, as determined by classroom observation data. Using these data is a second method of conducting a needs assessment, albeit in this case you are not seeking staff input on ideas for

Table 8.2 Walkthrough Results (Tabular Form)		
Look-fors	**Tally**	**Percentage**
Differentiation	43	50.0
Positive Reinforcement	8	9.3
Bellringer	12	14.0
Question Technique	23	26.7

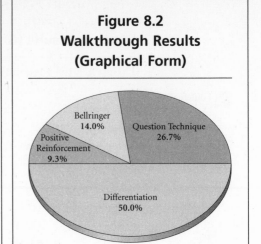

Figure 8.2 Walkthrough Results (Graphical Form)

professional development. Rather, you are actively gathering evidence in order to determine what needs exist or what areas you should focus on.

For example, the administrative team could develop a list of specific behaviors, practices, techniques, and strategies that you should expect to see during walkthroughs. On the basis of this list of "look-fors," you would then create a walkthrough tool that would allow you to record observed evidence (or lack thereof). After a specified number of walkthroughs have been conducted, you should have a reasonable sample of data with which to determine the frequencies of classroom practices and your teachers' need for improvement. Then, after tallying the occurrences of "Needs Improvement" from the walkthrough form, you would enter the results in a spreadsheet that contains each item from the team's walkthrough form. The look-fors found to have the greatest frequency of needing improvement would then be the focus for professional development. For example, as shown in Table 8.2 and Figure 8.2, over the course of eighty-six walkthroughs, there were forty-three occurrences where differentiation was indicated as needing improvement. These data could then be shared with the faculty to explain the rationale for providing professional development in the area of differentiation.

Learn in Context

Whether your area of focus for professional development has been solicited or prescribed, as we explain in the previous section, you must provide your staff with an opportunity to engage in deep learning. That can be accomplished by giving staff members opportunities to learn in context, as Fullan (2008) argues. Too often professional development falls short because teachers are not given a chance to learn and experiment with new strategies in context. Fullan explains that "professional development or courses, even when they are good in themselves, are removed from the setting in which teachers work. At best they represent useful input, but only that" (2008, p. 86). In other words, teachers shouldn't learn in isolation from their environment—their classrooms.

This kind of contextual learning can take the form of peer observations or coaching. In our experience, it is effective for teachers to regularly observe their colleagues—teachers not only in their department or on their team but also in other departments that have a very different content area—implementing the following:

- General instructional strategies
- Content-specific strategies
- Integration of reading, writing, and technology

There are certainly other look-fors your teachers can observe (classroom management, rapport building, questioning technique, and so on), but ultimately your teachers need to visit a variety of other teachers in order to be exposed to different ideas, philosophies, and practices. Although they can certainly learn from colleagues within their department or on their team, they might not readily think of observing a staff member from a different area because they might not have network connections with them, or the observations might be more difficult to coordinate.

Peer observation is "one of the ultimate acts of collaboration, as it requires teachers to make their actual teaching practice public to their colleagues and open to scrutiny" (Dana and Yendol-Hoppey, 2008, p. 36). It is also important because teachers "crave explicit demonstrations. . . . [M]ost of us want and need to see the approach in action" (Casey, 2011, p. 24). In observing a new instructional strategy, teachers "benefit from witnessing how students react to the content and the pedagogy and from imagining how it would go if [they] were teaching the lesson to [their] own students" (p. 24). Peer observations can also provide teachers nonevaluative support, which is distinctly different from what you offer when you enter the classroom as an administrator, regardless of how good your intentions are. For example, after a faculty or department meeting centering on an instructional strategy, if there is a department or team push to experiment with its implementation, then supportive feedback might best be offered by peers. If a department agrees that everyone will attempt to utilize the strategy within the next month, teachers can be paired to observe one another's execution, which enables them to offer their partners contextual, nonevaluative feedback.

Whether you devise your own plan for implementing peer observations or adapt the process that we explained more in depth in *How to Help Your School Thrive Without Breaking the Bank* (Gabriel and Farmer, 2009), the point is that you need to offer your assistance to your teachers and teacher leaders in ensuring that the specified number of peer observations actually occur over the course of the school year. That could take the form of following up with a teacher who has yet to observe a colleague, covering a class while a test is administered so that the teacher is free to observe someone, or helping arrange observations outside the department. Whatever form the assistance takes, your involvement is instrumental in helping peer observations take root. To better ensure the success of this practice, we offer the following tips to keep in mind when implementing peer observations:

- *Dedicate time.* Because teachers can learn so much from what they observe in other classrooms, it is worthwhile to dedicate your own instructional time to support this effort. For example, you might set aside some time at faculty meetings for teachers to share with other teachers, to debrief what they have observed, or even to launch another round of observations. By doing so, you demonstrate the value you place on the practice and your commitment to it.

- *Create a recording form.* There should be some kind of vehicle or format to help teachers structure the notes they take when visiting a classroom. To ensure more ownership of the process, engage your teachers in the development of their own checklist form, rather than simply giving them one. Once you have done this with a team of teachers, you can offer the list as a starting point for others by saying "this was created by another team of teachers."

- *Ensure dialogue.* There must be some kind of follow-up between teachers after the observation. If there is no opportunity for dialogue, then the practice of peer observation is almost an empty one. For them to process their experience and make meaning, teachers need to be able to ask clarifying and probing questions about what they observed and the choices that the demonstrating teacher made.

- *Allow for reflection.* Encourage your teachers to reflect on what they observe before actually meeting with the demonstrating teacher. It is important for them to have time to digest and thoughtfully process the various components and dimensions of what they observed.

Implement Systemic and Systematic Professional Development—Transform Faculty Meetings

To further complement the deep learning that is taking place in context, as we mentioned in the previous section, you should also implement regular learning opportunities for the entire faculty. As an administrative team, map out a professional development plan for the staff for the year—much as you would a curriculum—with components that would address areas of need and build on each other. Having these as regular events can help professional development become part of the overall school's culture. An easy place to implement this plan would be at faculty meetings.

The one or two days of dedicated professional development that most districts have in the summer serve as a good launching point for professional development topics that would then be sustained throughout the year during regular faculty meetings. It might seem sacrilegious to some to suggest this, because many schools' faculty meetings are centered on disseminating information and making announcements instead of being "times when everyone *learns,* not just when everyone *hears*" (Hoerr, 2005, p. 25). And even when faculty meetings purport to be centered on professional development, they are masquerading as such but only addressing such superficial issues as "the purpose of the guidance department" or "what you need to know about special education," or something that is really just informational in nature; they do not constitute the deep professional learning necessary to build capacity among teachers and improve student achievement. Rather, these are still information-based meetings during which teachers are passive participants and do not have the opportunity to learn and grow from and with one another.

If you hold monthly faculty meetings, you have built-in time to effectively organize and influence your school; capitalize on this possibility. If faculty meetings are not part of your building's culture, then the culture needs to change in order to have a systematic method of building capacity. Redesign these meetings so that they are ongoing conversations about teaching and learning. "These conversations move teaching from an individual pursuit to a group effort where there is ongoing help and support that promote learning and growth," and, more important, "When individual pursuits become group efforts, entire staffs expand their capacity to learn and teach and raise the quality of education offered students throughout the school" (Kohm and Nance, 2007, p. 229).

Design your faculty meetings much as you would a lesson. Identify your desired results and coordinate meaningful learning activities in which "the learning of both teachers and students can be addressed concurrently" (Kohm and Nance, 2007, p. 22) through what Lambert (2003) describes as surfacing of ideas, engaging in inquiry and reflection, and reshaping of current practices. And just as you would have your students direct their own learning and present what they've learned, include your teachers in the creation of staff development activities. Ultimately, these activities and discussions would then be continued at department and team meetings throughout the year in order to reinforce and sustain learning. Team and department meetings could be organized as study groups based on certain professional books or articles. Teachers would then use these study groups to "challenge and integrate their thinking and reach new levels of understanding . . . [and also] examine their assumptions about student learning" (Lambert, 2003, p. 14). To complement this learning, you could set up (or augment) a professional section in your school's library, and spiral back to these topics at your faculty meetings. The following are some guidelines to assist you when implementing professional development sessions during your faculty meetings:

Limit the Lecturing   Just as you discourage your teachers from relying heavily on lecturing in class, you should minimize the amount of talking at teachers that occurs during professional development sessions. When lecturing is the primary format, teachers are reduced to passive listeners who may not remain focused or retain the information. Moreover, lecturing sends a very hypocritical message: you encourage and expect your teachers to implement best practices in the classroom (and evaluate them accordingly), but then fail to practice what you claim to value. Further, lecturing (or reading slides verbatim from PowerPoints) is not aligned with "a core tenet of adult education: adults need to generate the content they are learning to be invested in it and to retain it longer" (Bambrick-Santoyo, 2010, p. 148). Bambrick-Santoyo also states that sessions where "the leader presents information, models its use, and then asks adults to use it" (p. 148) are not nearly as effective as what he calls "living the learning." He explains that "basketball players don't learn from a lecture; they learn on the court, living the directions given by the coach. Likewise, you don't learn to ride a bike by watching someone else do it; you have to get on and ride!" (p. 147). Therefore, you should strive to design all professional development for your staff such that it includes activities in which your teachers are able to make meaning on their own by developing their own observations and content and drawing their own conclusions, and provides opportunities for them to apply what they learned.

Form Purposeful Groups If you are going to have your teachers work collaboratively, we discourage you from allowing them to form their own groups. In these settings, your teachers are more inclined to sit "with the people they are closest to socially, but not necessarily the people that would add most value to their workshop experience" (Bambrick-Santoyo, 2010, p. 165). Also, you want to minimize the impact of negative, difficult, or resistant teachers (and let's face it—all faculties have them), so it is important to place them strategically into predetermined groups. To further maximize the groups' effectiveness, you should be sure to place a leader in each group, whether he or she is a formal leader, such as a department chair, or an informal leader whom people value and trust. It is important to have someone who can rise to the occasion, facilitate the work of the group, and provide proper influence when necessary.

Maximize the Time Just as you might urge teachers to maximize their instructional time, the same advice is even more important for you: teachers can easily sense when an inordinate amount of time is spent on "think-pair-share" or small group discussion—they'll see these activities as fluff or time-killers. Maximize the time you have your teachers assembled by ensuring that smooth transitions, clear directions, and minimal downtime are the norm; you will earn their respect by actively demonstrating that you value their time. And as a final piece of advice, overplan: to help you avoid the pitfalls we've mentioned, you should overplan based on the time you have with your teachers.

Give Them Takeaways Whatever you decide to do with your teachers, it needs to be practical. Regardless of the topic of the staff development session, your teachers need to leave that session discussing how valuable and worthwhile it was and how it will help their practice. Honor their time by providing them with takeaways—practical strategies that they can use on their own. For example, rather than simply presenting information about autism, offer them concrete strategies for how to work more effectively with autistic students. Or if it is necessary to present only information, avoid merely relying on a PowerPoint; instead, deliver the information through an instructional strategy, such as Jigsaw, that your teachers can use in their classrooms. In this two-for-one scenario, they receive the important information but also walk away with another tool for their repertoire of instructional strategies.

Follow Up   A good teacher will always circle back to see how his students have fared on a particular concept. This should be no different for you as an administrator: you are a teacher of teachers, so you need to check back in with them to gauge their success and their problems in implementing a new classroom strategy. You might even model sound instruction through spiraling, by revisiting previous staff development topics at the start of a new session to check for understanding and to reinforce them.

PROVIDE SUPPORT FOR COLLABORATIVE TEAMS

Another important way to increase teacher capacity is to increase the efficacy of your teachers in their work together, in terms of both process and content—how they function together and what they should collectively focus on. For example, many administrators have their teachers working in collaborative teams rather than in isolation because they recognize the benefit of coordinating their efforts to improve teaching and learning. However, even when time is dedicated during the contract day for teachers to work together, there are some common obstacles that can impede the effectiveness of collaborative teams. Whether there is a lack of structure or an unclear understanding of what should be occurring or how to make things happen, many collaborative teams ultimately end up just spinning their wheels or at worst focusing on trivial rather than substantive matters. Your administrative responsibility, then, is to guide your teachers, directly or indirectly through their teacher leaders, in how to work as an effective team and then in what work they should be doing.

Develop Norms

To form highly effective collaborative teams, your teachers will need to understand why they are being asked to collaborate. We've worked in schools where it was difficult for administrators to gain true buy-in from their staff because there was no clear understanding as to *why* they were expected to collaborate. Helping your teachers understand the "why" is essential to their working as a team, and, in many schools, it is never explained that the "degree to which people are working together in a coordinated, focused effort is a major determinant of the effectiveness of any organization" (DuFour, DuFour, Eaker, and Many, 2006, p. 107). So in making that case, you might choose to share professional literature about the value of collaborative teams or to explain how they have been "cited repeatedly in organizational literature as the most powerful structure for promoting the essential interdependence of an effective enterprise" (pp. 107–108). If your teachers are accustomed to working in isolation, it is imperative that you impress upon them that the "very reason any organization is established is to bring people together in an organized way to achieve a collective purpose that cannot be accomplished by working alone" (p. 107).

Teachers' working together does not necessarily translate into improvement in teaching and learning. This is through no fault of their own. In many cases, no one has showed them *how* they should be working and *what* they should be working on. In other cases, behaviors that surface during meetings prevent work from occurring or detract from the main focus. Or, more specifically, a lack of clear, acceptable behaviors and commitment to focus diminishes teachers' ability to harness their collective skills and talents. In other words, there must guidelines, or norms, in place that govern meetings; establishing norms can "help clarify expectations, promote open dialogue, and serve as a powerful tool for holding members accountable" (DuFour, DuFour, Eaker, and Many, 2006, p. 111), or as Kohm and Nance (2007) succinctly explain, "norms are promises that group members make to one another about how they will work and learn together" (p. 233). It is your responsibility to help your teachers learn *how* to function effectively as a team.

The first step is to model your expectations. More specifically, if you expect your teachers to have structured meetings and processes, then you must be willing to demonstrate leadership in this area. Modeling, however, is *not* the same as prescribing norms and guidelines for your teachers to implement; that kind of rigid leadership would severely hamper the development of any kind of buy-in from your teachers if they are not able to make meaning for themselves. Along those lines, we are hesitant to dictate what the norms should be: your teams' group dynamics are different and unique, so the members need to decide, aided by your facilitation, what norms are necessary for them to function effectively as a team. To this end, you can present them with a *process* for creating norms for their teams. You can share at a faculty meeting how the administrative team established its norms, or you could meet with your teacher leaders to demonstrate your process; but however you do it, it must be clear that the school leadership team practices what it preaches.

To develop team norms, we have used a simple process of asking staff to reflect on meetings that they have attended throughout their career: What about them did they like? What did they dislike? Why? We've also asked them to identify how their team recognizes and addresses behavior that is disruptive to the team meeting processes. We then ask staff to either individually or collectively brainstorm responses for the bold statements. It can be helpful for team members to be able to see the collection of responses in the form of a table that can eventually reflect their agreed-on norms. Table 8.3 is an example.

Table 8.3
Meetings and Norms

Things I Don't Like About Meetings	Norms to Address These Things
People want to discuss random issues at our meetings.	We will keep all discussions focused on agenda items only.
I don't like meetings that have no outcomes.	We will end each meeting by listing action items.

Things That Make Meetings Run Well	Norms to Protect These
When I know what the meeting is going to be about in advance.	We will send meeting agendas out one day in advance of each meeting.

A Norm to Address a Breach of Norms

We will have our meeting norms printed on the bottom of all agendas. When a norm is broken, we will use the agenda as a hand fan to indicate that our norms are being broken and to get back to meeting with our norms being honored.

We recommend developing a norm that speaks to a breach of norms because it is much easier to deal with a violation when it has already been discussed and the team has determined how it should be addressed prior to any breach. And to preserve the sanctity of the norms, so to speak, we even encourage teams to share the established norms with any visitor to a meeting and to hold him or her accountable to them as they would for any other stakeholder. Whether that visitor is a fellow teacher, an administrator, or even a visitor from the central office, he or she is expected to follow the norms of the team. Admittedly, we have been met with puzzled looks by some visitors, but their respect for the norms only adds credibility and validity to the team's commitments and processes.

Unpack or Unwrap Standards

Teachers are regularly exhorted to teach the standards that are in place in their state and school district. They hear this from politicians, the public, education experts, and perhaps even from you. But standards themselves do not ensure student learning. Standards are helpful to teachers only if teachers have a deep understanding of what the standard is actually saying about what they are expected to teach and students to learn. The process of gaining that understanding is often called unpacking or unwrapping standards.

Although we are not presenting a comprehensive perspective on unpacking standards, we would be remiss if we did not address this topic, because guiding your teacher leaders and teachers through a process they can use during department meetings or team collaboration time is another way to build their capacity. Through this unpacking process, teachers break down the standards to determine what each student must know, understand, and be able to do; as Ainsworth (2003) notes, "when teachers take the time to analyze each standard to identify its essential concepts and skills, the result is more effective instructional planning, assessment, and student learning" (p. 1). As important as this is to helping all students achieve, many teachers—and many administrators—are unfamiliar with unpacking standards and need guidance in this area.

Most states have standards that are so deeply layered and dense that Marzano and Hawstead (2008) claim it would take twenty-two years of schooling to cover them. Unpacking standards is thus "an opportunity to delete content that is not considered essential, delete content that is not amenable to classroom assessment, and combine content that is highly related" (p. 13). These are the steps to an unpacking process; we go into more detail following the list.

1. Identify the nouns and adjectives in the standard.

2. Record them in a category called "Stated Content" (Declarative Knowledge) —what you want your students to know.

3. Identify verbs in the standard.

4. Record them in a category called "Skills and Processes" (Procedural Knowledge)—what you want your students to be able to do.

5. Generate a list of information that is *implied* by the items in the Stated Content category and record them alongside that category.

6. Having identified content and process in the previous steps, state the "context" that they inform.

7. Pull back to view the bigger picture and impact in order to create "Connections."

The starting point in this process is to provide your teachers with hard copies of the standards so that they can mark them up when systematically dissecting the language used in the standards. Specifically, you are asking your teachers to identify the important nouns (and adjectives) and verbs in the particular standard. This process helps your teachers determine the learning goals "implied in any standard" (Jackson, 2009, p. 58). As Jackson explains, "The first type of goal is a content goal. Content goals emphasize content knowledge. Their main focus is on what students need to know or understand. The second type of goal is a process goal. Process goals focus on students' learning or developing a skill" (p. 58). Your teachers differentiate between these goals by focusing on the parts of speech in the standard: content is indicated by nouns and adjectives; process is signified by verbs (Ainsworth, 2003). In many standards, even though you have identified the content by singling out the nouns (or adjectives), there is also *implied* content, which is equally important as the stated content, both of which appear on high-stakes assessments; implied content is the information we associate with the stated content, although it often does not appear in the standard. Teachers generally find identifying the implied content to be an enjoyable activity, drawing on their own knowledge, state-released assessment items or questions from standardized tests, local curriculum guides, textbooks, and ancillary materials.

After teachers have identified the content goals (or declarative knowledge, in that it is something students must know) and the process goals (or procedural knowledge, what the student must be able to do) embedded in a particular standard, they then need to determine how these goals fit into the *context,* or the bigger picture of what is being studied. Ainsworth (2003) refers to context as the "Big Ideas," or the themes, perspectives, concepts, theories, and so on that teachers want their students to retain long after a particular unit of study has ended. Wiggins and McTighe (2005) characterize these Big Ideas as having "lasting value" (p. 66); they are centered more on what students need to know than on what is nice to know. Typically, it is "easier to identify the Big Ideas after the standards and indicators have been 'unwrapped' and represented on a graphic organizer, rather than trying to determine them from the original standards text," because it helps to see the progression from the concrete to the abstract (Ainsworth, 2003, p. 28). And because these concepts are expansive by nature and your teachers are working toward depth of knowledge rather than extent, there should not be a large number of them.

The unpacked standards and correlating main concepts are then organized around "overarching questions" that are the "conceptual pillars" for programs of study (Wiggins and McTighe, 2005, p. 114). These "essential questions" are not lesson objectives stated as simple queries; they are "not answerable with finality in a brief sentence. . . . Their aim is to stimulate thought, to provoke inquiry, and to spark more questions" (p. 106) that push you to "the heart of things—the essence" (p. 107). These open-ended questions are less about "what" (or fact recall) and more aligned with "how" and "why"; they are designed to provoke deep thought and critical thinking as well as provide focus for the unit of study. In essence, these are the *connections* that your teachers want their students to form between themselves and their lives and the concepts, materials, and even the discipline. And by having your teachers identify enduring understandings and essential questions, you are also helping them identify what matters most, or, as Ainsworth (2003) refers to them, Power Standards, "since all standards and indicators are *not* of equal importance" (p. 23).

After teachers have underlined nouns and circled verbs as Ainsworth advises, it is helpful to chart their work in a graphic organizer to create an overall picture of the standard. An additional benefit of having this kind of tangible product is that it can serve as an added support for teachers new to a department or new to teaching. Some teachers might prefer a concept map, others some kind of chart. The format is not as important as having some sort of visual aid and a systematic process that clearly and accurately organizes the information in an easy-to-understand way. Your teachers could work through this process individually, but we suggest that they work in pairs and then compare their findings with others on the team; or, if they are just beginning this kind of work, they could tackle a few standards as a team to get a handle on the process.

After your teachers have completed this exercise, they should have some kind of takeaway—either a hierarchal bulleted list, a concept map, or a graphic organizer—that they can use on their own. Table 8.4 is an example of a standard for World History and Geography to 1500 AD from the Virginia Standards of

---

Table 8.4
Unpacking a Standard

Standard: WHI.13 The student will demonstrate knowledge of developments leading to the Renaissance in Europe in terms of its impact on Western civilization by

a. identifying the economic foundations of the Italian Renaissance;

b. sequencing events related to the rise of Italian city-states and their political development, including Machiavelli's theory of governing as described in *The Prince*;

c. citing artistic, literary, and philosophical creativity, as contrasted with the medieval period, including Leonardo da Vinci, Michelangelo, and Petrarch;

d. comparing the Italian and the Northern Renaissance, and citing the contributions of writers.

Declarative Knowledge		Procedural Knowledge	
Nouns and Adjectives (Know and Understand)		Verbs (Be Able to Do)	
Stated Content	**Implied Content**	**Skills**	
Italian Renaissance Economic foundations of the Italian Renaissance	• Crusades • Demand • Usury • Credit	Identify	Identify economic foundations of the Italian Renaissance.

Table 8.4 *(continued)*

Rise and political development of Italian city-states	• Florence, Venice, and Genoa • Trading centers • Independent city-states	Sequence	Sequence events related to the rise of Italian city-states and their economic development.
Machiavelli • *The Prince* • Theory of governing	• Supports absolute power • "The ends justify the means"	Describe	Describe Machiavelli's theory of governing in *The Prince*.
Artistic, literary, and philosophical creativity • Leonardo da Vinci • Michelangelo • Petrarch	 • *Mona Lisa* • *Last Supper* • Sistine Chapel ceiling • *David* • Sonnets	Cite Contrast	Cite artistic, literary, and philosophical creativity. Contrast artistic, literary, and philosophical creativity with the medieval period.
Northern Renaissance	Merged Christianity with humanism	Compare	Compare the Italian and Northern Renaissance.
Contributions of writers	• Erasmus: *The Praise of Folly* • Sir Thomas More: *Utopia* • Movable-type printing press made production of books (Gutenberg Bible) cheaper and helped spread ideas	Cite	Cite the contributions of writers.

(continued)

Table 8.4 *(continued)*

Context (Big Ideas)
The political systems and cultural expressions created during the Renaissance demonstrate the declining influence of the Catholic Church and a growing belief in human ability and potential.
The political, social, and economic changes that took place during the Renaissance were made possible by interactions with other cultures, especially in the Middle East.

Connections (Essential Questions)
How did the events of the Renaissance contribute to the growth of secularism and an increased emphasis on humanism in political systems and cultural expressions?
How did Europe's interactions with other cultures affect its political, economic, and social systems?

Learning for World History I (http://www.doe.virginia.gov/testing/sol/standards _docs/history_socialscience/index.shtml#sol) and how all these pieces organized together can look for your teachers.

The next step is to have your teachers create an assessment to determine if the students have learned the standards that they have unpacked. This is in contrast to the more typical approach, in which teachers develop their assessments when they near the end of a unit of study: they reflect back on what was taught and develop a test that reflects that. And they begin their planning process by selecting topics (*To Kill a Mockingbird* and theme, for example) and activities (guided reading, journal writes, collaborative work) for the unit of study. Instead, what you are having your teachers do with this strategy is identify in advance, before instruction actually begins, what students must be able to know and do, or the desired results, and also how their learning will be measured. Only after having identified their results and the assessments will teachers begin to discuss what activities and topics they will use as vehicles to help facilitate the transfer of learning. What you are helping your teachers do is what Wiggins and McTighe (2005) refer to as *backwards design,* or having your teachers begin with the end in mind, which, as Covey (1989) explains, is starting "with a clear understanding of your destination. It means to know where you're going so that you better understand where you are now so that the steps you take are always in the right direction" (p. 98).

Review Data

Even in today's era of accountability and high-stakes assessments, there are still teachers who are unfamiliar with analyzing test data. If you have teachers on your staff who fall into this category, it is important that you show them in a non-threatening and supportive way how to review and analyze data. As data are the "cornerstone of all your improvement efforts" (Gabriel and Farmer, 2009, p. 200), helping your teachers learn how to analyze them is also another way to build your teachers' capacity.

The value in reviewing data is that the results can be used to help your teams work together on common goals and trust each other to reach those goals. The data provide evidence of the actual effects of teachers' efforts, instead of merely their good intentions. DuFour, DuFour, Eaker, and Many (2006) suggest that teams working on "goals will focus on the intended outcome rather than on the strategies to achieve the outcome" (p. 159). To achieve an intended outcome, teams must determine a plan of action by reviewing specific data, such as data on student achievement, and making meaning out of the data. The following is a process you could use to lead your teacher teams through their review of data to make meaning of the results from a district benchmark or a team-developed common assessment:

1. Looking at the assessment results, each teacher identifies the three questions their own students missed most frequently.

2. Each teacher then identifies the skills associated with each frequently missed question.

3. The teachers then compare their results with each other to determine if there is a common pattern among the incorrect answers. (Are students picking the same incorrect answer? and so on.)

4. In searching for a common pattern, the teachers then examine these frequently missed questions to determine if there was an issue with the content, vocabulary, question structure, or some combination of these.

5. If the assessment being reviewed is a districtwide one, then compare the team's results with those of the district to see if they run parallel or if there is an acceptable degree of difference.

6. If the content, vocabulary, or structure were not problematic on the questions that were most frequently missed, then the teachers need to identify potential causes for the low performance on each question or skill area (or both).

After your teachers have had the opportunity to examine the assessment instrument and the student results, you need to emphasize an important final step: developing an action plan to serve the students' needs.

DEVELOP OTHER LEADERS

Another way to build capacity among your teachers is to develop their leadership capabilities. In some schools, developing leaders is an expectation, a stated responsibility; however, in many other schools, it is unstated or, worse yet, overlooked, as administrative focus and attention are limited only to what occurs in the classroom. This concept is so crucial to an organization's success that some corporations, such as Intel, GE, and Shell, expect CEOs and other leaders to develop new leaders within the company (Cohen and Tichy, 1997). We contend that what we call *growing leaders* (Gabriel and Farmer, 2009, p. 39)—developing your teachers' leadership abilities—is as important a responsibility as building your teachers' instructional capacity. Growing leaders

- Reduces stagnation
- Increases retention
- Provides organizational stability
- Ensures smooth succession
- Increases professional growth
- Broadens perspectives
- Increases loyalty
- Promotes shared values
- Distributes work

- Shares a vision

- Involves the stakeholders

- Advances commitment

Probably the most important benefit, though, is that "leaders developing leaders multiply their effect" (Fullan, 2010, p. 75).

It is important to note that the value of mentoring relationships is not one-sided, heavily favoring only the mentee. You and your staff members will be able to learn with and from one another, trade strategies, console and empathize with each other, and even set goals together for growth and achievement in a certain area. In addition, once a leader starts to mentor someone, he will more likely hold himself more accountable for his own behaviors, actions, and practices. Most important, developing other leaders can be an enriching and rewarding experience—even "rejuvenating," as Alvy and Robbins (1998, p. 10) note—not just for mentors but for your future leaders as well.

In our own schools, developing leaders is a standard for the principal, assistant principals, department chairs, and team leaders. Each person in these leadership positions is expected to identify a staff member who has leadership potential or has expressed an interest in leadership and to mentor her, developing her leadership base. This mentoring does not necessarily assume a formalized process, but the mentee would be expected to fill in or act as a backup during the mentor's absence. The mentor would also create some learning opportunities for the mentee to handle in his absence and then debrief about them later. Ideally, the mentor would attempt to expose his mentee to some of his responsibilities and work when he is in the building as well. A critical aspect of developing leadership capacity in this respect is creating the time to talk with mentees—making yourself available to discuss what was observed, role-play situations, and ask and answer questions.

Building your teachers' capacity can be one of the more difficult and challenging aspects of being an administrator. Paradoxically, though, it can also be one of the more rewarding and enriching experiences. Just as when you were a classroom teacher you enjoyed seeing your students learn and grow, helping your teachers develop professionally and expand their knowledge base and repertoire of skills can be an equally gratifying experience. We attribute this partially to what we believe is a simple truth: educators become administrators because they want to improve learning for students, to help them achieve more in the classroom and in life. By improving the quality of teaching, administrators are able to accomplish that goal. But we also believe that building your teachers' capacity is a satisfying responsibility because ultimately you are serving as a teacher; you are instructing and facilitating learning. Doing so is appealing because although your title may be that of administrator, at heart you are still a teacher, and building capacity satisfies the most basic desire of all teachers: to help other people grow.

Conclusion:
Beyond the Tough Stuff

You serve as a school administrator because of your desire to help others, and your sense of responsibility to them. We specifically use the word "serve" not solely in the sense of acting as an administrator but rather as more aligned with the idea that you *serve* students, staff, and parents. As we hope you've gleaned from this book, school administration is deeply rooted not only in relationships but also in the notion of *servant leadership,* a term first coined by Robert K. Greenleaf (1977). In this practice, your main focus is on the people with whom you work. As a servant leader, you tend to their problems and development. Their needs are your needs because you put the people you serve ahead of yourself. Although you might lead them, you are paradoxically subservient to them.

As an administrator, you build relationships with your stakeholders to help them grow and, ultimately, to increase student learning. Of course, preparing a budget, approving a field trip, or completing some other administrative task does ultimately have an impact on students, but it is those other actions you engage in that help students and teachers achieve more and improve themselves. It is in this area that you find yourself most functioning as a servant leader. Whether helping students learn the essential skills of state and common core standards or helping them learn who they are, who they want to and should become, and how to work with others, you cannot possibly help adolescents grow socially, emotionally, and academically without devoting a part of yourself to them and their needs.

Working with parents and teachers is no different: you serve them as well, yet in different capacities. Parents are your clients too, an important part of the equation for student success, and you serve them indirectly in that their children are your number-one priority. You also serve them directly because cultivating a relationship with them and being responsive to them and their needs are essential tasks. You serve your staff members in that you attend to them, assist them, and guide them, all in the service of helping them improve and grow as people and as professionals. Because your teachers might not immediately or always see your actions in this light (which complicates your role and the task each year), it's important to keep in the forefront of your mind that everything you are doing is not for you but for them. If you are effective in your efforts, everything you do in the service of your teachers will consequently prove to be of great service to others, and in return you will become much better at what you do as an administrator.

As demanding as it can sometimes be to serve others as well as handle a host of other responsibilities inherent to your job, school administration is also a satisfying and enriching experience. Many students might not now enjoy receiving discipline for an infraction, but it is incredibly satisfying when that same student comes to you later and not only admits to having needed that type of discipline but also thanks you for it, acknowledging that you did the right thing. You built a rapport with him and demonstrated that you would never give up on him no matter how many times he was sent to your office. Or perhaps he cites something you said that struck a chord and stayed with him over the years; you might not even be able to recall now whatever it was you said, but its impact was life changing—possibly even lifesaving—for this young person. Or it could be that a parent thanks you for all of your efforts and hard work, or keeps you updated on her child's progress after he has left your school, or writes a letter to your supervisor detailing how you always put her child first, never giving up on him no matter how difficult the situation or his behavior became. Or perhaps it is the teacher who shares with you the success he is currently experiencing in the classroom because of the time you took to talk with him about his professional practices and to help him enhance them. Maybe that teacher was at first not as open to your suggestions and conversations, but he later came to understand and appreciate your perspective and motivation in working with him. That is when the tough stuff ceases to be so and instead transforms into rewarding moments and future opportunities to make an impact.

But perhaps one of the most enriching aspects of being a school administrator is serving your fellow administrators. Sharing your own knowledge (or what you have gained from this book) with an aspiring administrator, a novice, or even a veteran can be rejuvenating. Such sharing makes a positive impact in your field and helps keep you and your position fresh. We've each benefited personally from administrators who took the time to mentor us and share their frontline knowledge and experiences with us; we understand how gratifying it is to be able to do that because we've been fortunate to have the same opportunities ourselves.

Our profession is indeed a rewarding one. Certainly there will be times when you are tried and taxed beyond what you think you can handle: the tough stuff can drain you and lead you to question how much more you can take. We offer you the consolation that everyone has been there. Our hope is that this book makes your time in that place a little easier to manage so that you can continue to make a difference in the lives of your students, parents, and teachers.

REFERENCES

Abrams, J. *Having Hard Conversations.* Thousand Oaks, Calif.: Corwin Press, 2009.

Ainsworth, L. *"Unwrapping" the Standards: A Simple Process to Make Standards Manageable.* Englewood, Colo.: Advanced Learning Press, 2003.

Alvy, H. B., and Robbins, P. *If I Only Knew: Success Strategies for Navigating the Principalship.* Thousand Oaks, Calif.: Corwin Press, 1998.

Bambrick-Santoyo, P. *Driven by Data: A Practical Guide to Improve Instruction.* San Francisco: Jossey-Bass, 2010.

Bondy, E., and Ross, D. D. "The Teacher as Warm Demander." *Educational Leadership,* 2008, *66*(1), 54–58.

Boynton, M., and Boynton, C. *The Educator's Guide to Preventing and Solving Discipline Problems.* Alexandria, Va.: ASCD, 2005.

Brooks, M. "Parents as Partners." *Principal Leadership,* 2011, *12*(2), 24–27.

"Bullying, Cyberbullying and the Schools." *School Leadership Briefing,* Dec. 1, 2010. http://www.schoolbriefing.com/532/bullying-cyberbullying-and-the-schools/.

Casey, K. "Modeling Lessons." *Educational Leadership,* 2011, *69*(2), 24–29.

Cohen, E., and Tichy, N. "How Leaders Develop Leaders." *Training & Development,* May 1997. http://www.noeltichy.com/HowLeadersDevelopLeaders.pdf.

Covey, S. *The 7 Habits of Highly Effective People.* New York: Simon & Schuster, 1989.

Curwin, R., Mendler, A. N., and Mendler, B. D. *Discipline with Dignity: New Challenges, New Solutions.* (3rd ed.) Alexandria, Va.: ASCD, 2008.

Dana, N. F., and Yendol-Hoppey, D. *The Reflective Educator's Guide to Professional Development: Coaching Inquiry-Oriented Learning Communities.* Thousand Oaks, Calif.: Corwin Press, 2008.

Daresh, J. C. *Beginning the Assistant Principalship: A Practical Guide for New School Administrators.* Thousand Oaks, Calif.: Corwin Press, 2004.

Davis, K. "Management Communication and the Grapevine." In S. Ferguson and S. Ferguson (eds.), *Organizational Communication.* (2nd ed.) New Brunswick, N.J.: Transaction, 1988.

DuFour, R., DuFour, R., Eaker, R., and Many, T. *Learning by Doing: A Handbook for Professional Learning Communities at Work.* Bloomington, Ind.: Solution Tree, 2006.

Evans, R. *Seven Secrets of the Savvy School Leader: A Guide to Surviving and Thriving*. San Francisco: Jossey-Bass, 2010.

Fiore, D. J. *Introduction to Educational Administration*. New York: Eye on Education, 2004.

Fullan, M. *The Six Secrets of Change: What the Best Leaders Do to Help Their Organizations Survive and Thrive*. San Francisco: Jossey-Bass, 2008.

Fullan, M. *Motion Leadership: The Skinny on Becoming Change Savvy*. Thousand Oaks, Calif.: Corwin Press, 2010.

Gabriel, J. G., and Farmer, P. C. *How to Help Your School Thrive Without Breaking the Bank*. Alexandria, Va.: ASCD, 2009.

Gladwell, M. *Blink*. New York: Back Bay Books, 2005.

Goodwin, B. "Bullying Is Common—and Subtle." *Educational Leadership*, 2011, *69*(1), 82–83.

Greene, R. W. "Calling All Frequent Flyers." *Educational Leadership*, 2010, *68*(2), 28–34.

Greenleaf, R. K. *Servant Leadership: A Journey into the Nature of Legitimate Power and Greatness*. New York: Paulist Press, 1977.

Griffin, J. *How to Say It at Work: Putting Yourself Across with Power Words, Phrases, Body Language, and Communication Secrets*. Paramus, N.J.: Prentice Hall, 1998.

Hoerr, T. *The Art of Leadership*. Alexandria, Va.: ASCD, 2005.

Jackson, R. *Never Work Harder Than Your Students and Other Great Principles of Teaching*. Alexandria, Va.: ASCD, 2009.

Johnson, D. W., and Johnson, R. T. *Reducing School Violence Through Conflict Resolution*. Alexandria, Va.: ASCD, 1995.

Kohm, B., and Nance, B. *Principals Who Learn: Asking the Right Questions, Seeking the Best Solutions*. Alexandria, Va.: ASCD, 2007.

Lambert, L. *Leadership Capacity for Lasting School Improvement*. Alexandria, Va.: ASCD 2003.

Marzano, R. J., and Hawstead, M. W. *Making Standards Useful in the Classroom*. Alexandria, Va.: ASCD, 2008.

Marzano, R. J., Marzano, J. S., and Pickering, D. J. *Classroom Management That Works: Research-Based Strategies for Every Teacher*. Alexandria, Va.: ASCD, 2003.

Marzano, R. J., and Pickering, D. J., with Heflebower, T. *The Highly Engaged Classroom*. Bloomington, Ind.: Marzano Research Laboratory, 2010.

McCarthy, M. M., Cambron-McCabe, N. H., and Thomas, S. B. *Public School Law: Teachers' and Students' Rights*. (4th ed.) Needham Heights, Mass.: Allyn & Bacon, 1998.

McLeod, J., Fisher, J., and Hoover G. *The Key Elements of Classroom Management: Managing Time and Space, Student Behavior, and Instructional Strategies*. Alexandria, Va.: ASCD, 2003.

Mendler, A. N. *Connecting with Students*. Alexandria, Va.: ASCD, 2001.

MetLife. *MetLife Survey of the American Teacher: Transitions and the Role of Supportive Relationships, 2004–2005*. http://www.eric.ed.gov/PDFS/ED488837.pdf.

Munger, L., and von Frank, V. *Change, Lead, Succeed: Building Capacity with School Leadership Teams.* Oxford, Ohio: National Staff Development Council, 2010.

Patterson, K., Grenny, J., McMillan, R., and Switzler, A. *Crucial Conversations: Tools for Talking When Stakes Are High.* New York: McGraw-Hill, 2002.

Reason, C. *Leading a Learning Organization: The Science of Working with Others.* Bloomington, Ind.: Solution Tree, 2009.

Rodkin, P. C. "Bullying—and the Power of Peers." *Educational Leadership*, 2011, *69*(1), 10–16. http://www.ascd.org/publications/educational-leadership/sept11/vol69/num01/Bullying%E2%80%94And-the-Power-of-Peers.aspx.

Rutherford, P. *Instruction for All Students.* Alexandria, Va.: Just Ask Publications, 2002.

Simpson, P. R. *Assistant Principal's Survival Guide: Practical Guidelines & Materials for Managing All Areas of Your Work.* Paramus, N.J.: Prentice Hall, 2000.

Smith, R., and Lambert, M. "Assuming the Best." *Educational Leadership*, 2008, *66*(1), 16–21.

Ury, W. *Getting Past No: Negotiating Your Way from Confrontation to Cooperation.* New York: Bantam Books, 1993.

Watkins, M. *The First 90 Days: Critical Success Strategies for New Leaders at All Levels.* Boston: Harvard Business School Press, 2003.

Wiggins, G., and McTighe, J. *Understanding by Design, Expanded 2nd Edition.* Alexandria, Va.: ASCD, 2005.

Wlodkowski, R. J. *Motivational Opportunities for Successful Teaching.* Phoenix: Universal Dimensions, 1983.

INDEX

Page references followed by *fig* indicate an illustrated figure; followed by *t* indicate a table.

A

B

Bambrick-Santoyo, P., 138, 139

Behaviors: comparing attitudes to, 125t; don't focus on attitudes but on, 124–126; give apologies followed by changed, 124; monitoring conversations by assessing, 120–121; understanding reasons for difficult or resistant, 124. *See also* Student misbehavior

Blaming language, 8–9

Blink (Gladwell), 84

Bluffing, 58

Body language: during discussion of the referral, 58; "the look" (or "hairy eyeball"), 37, 58; mediation ground rule regarding, 9; monitoring staff conversation, 121–122. *See also* Language

Bondy, E., 35

Boredom, 30

Boundaries: establishing parent conference, 106; misbehavior due to lack of, 31–32

Boynton, C., 15, 17, 20, 21, 28, 32, 37

Boynton, M., 15, 17, 20, 21, 28, 32, 37

Brooks, M., 88

Building capacity: challenges and rewards of, 151–152; developing other leaders for, 150–151; importance of continuous development and, 129–130; maintaining focus on deep learning for, 130–140; professional development for, 130–140; providing support for collaborative teams for, 140–150; scenario on need for, 129. *See also* Teachers

Building rapport, 35–36

Bullies: four parenting practices that can create, 21; meeting with the, 19–20; "socially connected," 16; talking with the parents of the, 21; traditional view of, 16; who are also victimized, 16

Bullycide, description of, 14

Bullying: description of, 5; physical, 17; providing students safety from, 59–60; understanding seriousness of, 15–16; verbal, 16–17; widespread incidence of, 14–15. *See also* Cyberbullying; Student conflict types

"Bullying, Cyberbullying and the Schools" (Swearer), 16

Bullying responses: to cyberbullying, 22–23; meeting with the bully, 19–20; meeting with the victim, 18; talking with bully's parents, 21; talking with the victim's parents, 18–19

C

Cafeteria, eating with students in the, 42

Cambron-McCabe, N. H., 66

Casey, K., 135

Child pornography, 23

Child Protective Services, 23, 94

Class rules, 35

Classroom Management That Works (Marzano, Marzano, and Pickering), 28

Classroom misbehavior: minimizing, 32–39; scenario on time spent dealing with, 27–28; understanding, 30–32. *See also* Infractions

Classroom misbehavior causes: alienation, 31; because they can, 32; boredom, 30; drug or alcohol abuse, 30–31; to earn creditability with peers, 31; home life, 31; lack of boundaries, 31–32; lack of skills, 30; personality conflict, 32; quest for attention, 31; sense of entitlement, 31; work avoidance, 30

Classrooms: accompanying student back following referral, 59; employ proximity and mobility in, 34–35; establishing clear procedures and routines in, 34; move student seats when necessary, 37; reward systems used in, 38; rules of the, 35. *See also* Schools

Clementi, T., 17

Cluster chain grapevine, 127

Cohen, E., 150

Collaborative teams: analyzing test data, 149–150; developing norms for, 140–142; increasing teacher capacity through, 140; reviewing desired meeting norms, 142t; unpacking or unwrapping standards, 143–149

Commitments. *See* Staff commitments

Communication: body language, 9, 37, 58, 121–122; calling parents to minimize student misbehavior, 36–37; of classroom procedures and routines, 34; navigating issues related to staff, 111–128; when to use strong language in, 122–123. *See also* Language; Parent conferences; Referral discussion

Community involvement, 96

Conflicts: accept as possibility in staff communication, 122–123; bullying and cyberbullying, 5, 15–23; student, 6–14, 61–77; student-teacher, 23–24

Connecting with students: importance and benefits of, 40–41; reconnecting following suspension, 76–77; techniques for, 41–42

Consequences: attune with school policies, 46; give students a reason for the, 57; mediation establishment of future, 13; minimizing student misbehavior by giving, 38. *See also* Discipline

Contextual learning: peer observation form of, 135–137; professional development through, 134–135

Conversation guidelines. *See* Staff conversation guidelines

Covey, S., 148–149

Credibility: demonstrating respect for students to improve your, 41; how bluffing can damage your, 58; student misbehavior to create peer, 31

Curwin, R., 32, 35, 59, 60, 88

Cyberbullying: description of, 5; legalities of when you can respond to, 22–23; responding to, 22–23; understanding seriousness of, 17. *See also* Bullying

Cyberbullying responses: considerations for, 22; legalities related to, 22–23; teaching about cyberbullying, 23

D

Dana, N. F., 135

Daresh, J. C., 46, 54

Data analysis, 149–150

Davis, K., 126, 127

Discipline: addressing concerns following administration of, 72–77; administration time spent on, 28–29; developing a philosophy regarding, 46; discussion with your staff on, 29–39; give students a reason for the, 57; multiple meanings and aspects of, 45–46; reviewing the discipline data, 39–40; scenario on dealing with student, 45. *See also* Consequences; Infractions; Referrals; Student misbehavior

Discipline discussion: on minimizing student misbehavior, 32–39; on understanding classroom misbehavior, 30–32

Goodwin, B., 16

Google Docs, 132

Gossip: conflicts caused by, 4; grapevine chain of, 127

The grapevine: four types of operations of, 127; as informal channel of communication, 126; tapping, 127–128

Greene, R. W., 30

Greenleaf, R. K., 153

Grenny, J., 111, 123, 124, 128

Griffin, J., 121

Growing leaders: benefits of, 150–151; description of, 150

H

"Hairy eyeball" (or "the look"), 37, 58

Hawstead, M. W., 143

Heflebower, T., 34

The Highly Engaged Classroom (Marzano and Pickering, with Heflebower), 34

Hoerr, T., 137

Home life situation, 31

Home visits, 96

How to Help Your School Thrive Without Breaking the Bank (Gabriel and Farmer), 136

I

"I Heard It Through the Grapevine" (song), 126

Infractions: during discussion don't focus solely on the, 54–55; emphasize that behavior was a poor choice, 51–52; investigating, 61–77; referrals received for, 45, 47–55. *See also* Classroom misbehavior; Discipline; Student misbehavior

Instruction for All Students (Rutherford), 34

Intel, 150

Investigation: addressing postdiscipline concerns, 72–77; description of, 61–62; managing your, 62–72. *See also* Fact finding

Investigation management: documenting evidence, 71; get coverage for your other duties, 62; interviewing students, 65; making parental contact, 71; process and legalities of searching students, 66–71; reporting to the police, 72; securing statements from teacher or staff witnesses, 61–62; taking statements from student witnesses, 63–64

J

Jackson, R., 144

Johnson, D. W., 11, 24

Johnson, R. T., 11, 24

K

Kohm, B., 141

Kounin, J., 35

L

Lambert, M., 36

Language: abusive, 106; blaming, 8–9; discrepancies between verbal and body, 121; ground rules for mediating student conflicts regarding, 7–9; professional or personal attack, 8, 107; sarcastic, 37–38; verbal bullying, 16–17; when to use strong, 122–123. *See also* Body language; Communication

Learning environment: how student misbehavior can impact, 42–43; importance of a positive, 24–25; offering teachers strategies for orderly, 34; responding to cyberbullying as disruption of, 22; responsibility to